GRACE

W9-CLJ-654

THE LIFE OF
GRACE

FOUNDATIONS OF CATHOLIC THEOLOGY SERIES

Gerard S. Sloyan, *Editor*

THE LIFE OF GRACE

P. GREGORY STEVENS, OSB

The Catholic University of America
Washington, D.C.

PRENTICE-HALL, INC.
Englewood Cliffs, N.J.

1963

Nihil Obstat:

Bernard Theall, OSB
Censor Deputatus

Imprimatur:

✠ Patrick A. O'Boyle, DD
Archbishop of Washington
September 19, 1962

PRENTICE-HALL INTERNATIONAL, INC., *London*
PRENTICE-HALL OF AUSTRALIA, PTY., LTD., *Sydney*
PRENTICE-HALL OF CANADA, LTD., *Toronto*
PRENTICE-HALL FRANCE, S.A.R.L., *Paris*
PRENTICE-HALL OF JAPAN, INC., *Tokyo*
PRENTICE-HALL DE MEXICO, S.A., *Mexico City*

C

EDITOR'S NOTE

This series offers the depth and richness of the divine message of salvation proclaimed to us by Christ. The theology, or "faith seeking understanding," contained here is not on a catechetical level, nor yet on a complex, higher level; it is clear and nontechnical, but at the same time adult and thorough. It is a scholarly presentation of revelation.

These volumes do not adopt an apologetic approach. They

neither attempt to justify Catholic faith nor aim at convincing those who do not profess it of the reasonableness of believing. This series is written primarily for those who already believe, who accept the Church as the living continuation of Christ, and the Scriptures as divinely inspired.

The authors do not attempt a philosophy of God or of Christianity, but a study of the mystery of God seen through the eyes of faith. The mystery of faith will not be dispelled by the study of these books. It will remain.

Since some background in philosophy on the part of the reader is needed, and cannot in every case be presumed, there are times when philosophical terms will need to be explained. Philosophical reasoning is very much a part of speculative theology.

Although the breakdown of the series is along traditional lines, each volume is designed to emphasize the oneness of God's plan of salvation and not its different facets. Distinction is made in order to unite. What is taught in the Scriptures is stressed, so that it may be seen how men of the Bible understood the message entrusted to them. The historical aspects of doctrine as held by Christians are then treated: the testimony of the early Christian writers and the liturgy to the belief of the Church; the controversies and heresies that necessitated defense and precise formulation, and finally, the magisterial teaching in each subject area. In this way speculative theology, or the present understanding of each mystery, is not seen in isolation from the sources of faith.

Thus, the revealed Christian message is viewed as the *tradition* (in the fullest and best sense of that theological term) expressed in and through the Church over the centuries—more explicitly formulated, from age to age, and with further applications. But it is still the same saving message begun in the Old Testament and perfected in the mystery and person of Jesus Christ.

One last point is important. Although the study of theology is an exercise of intellect, it can never be exclusively this. The message of Jesus Christ is a living Word, an invitation to participate in the saving event of the redemption, starting in this world by faith and the union of grace, and culminating in heaven by vision and immediate union. This invitation demands response or living faith. The study of the Christian message through theology requires such response, for the message is not something that was heard and assented to once. It is a Word addressed to us that requires our vigorous "Yes" for a lifetime.

CONTENTS

vii

CHAPTER THREE

SUMMARY OF THE THEOLOGY OF GRACE, *page 66*

APPENDIX

NOTE ON BAIUS AND JANSENIUS, *page 97*

THE LIFE OF
GRACE

CHAPTER ONE

THE NEW TESTAMENT

The doctrine of grace in the New Testament concerns the order of salvation established in Christ. Grace is essentially the new life communicated to man through him. By this new life man is freed from all that separates him from God and is united through the Spirit in Christ to the Father. The New Testament writers present the divine reality of grace as it is realized concretely in the individual Christian, under its various aspects. Whereas the synoptic gospels (Matthew, Mark, and Luke) emphasize the establishment of the kingdom through the person and deeds of Christ, St. John dwells on the Christian's participation in Christ who is light and life. St. Paul presents the whole panorama of grace as a liberation from sin and an incorporation into Christ. The Christian reader of the New Testament is made aware of the richness of the doctrine of grace by following its presentation in all its variety and unity.

THE SYNOPTIC GOSPELS

Grace: The Kingdom of the Father

The synoptic gospels present the reality of a loving Father in heaven. The Father, revealed indeed in the Old Testament as a God of majesty and as the loving Lord of the covenant with Israel, is now made known in the "fullness of time" through his Son. God is the almighty "Father in heaven [who] gives good things to those who ask him" (Mt 7,11), who "knows what you need" (Mt 6,8.32),[1] being concerned with the wellbeing of all his creatures. (Mt 10,29) Christ calls God his Father, but also directs us to see God as "our Father." (Mt 6,9.15) The essential feature of the reign of grace is a filial spirit in which through the mediation of Christ we address the sovereign God as truly a loving Father to us. Our life of grace is one of sonship: "Be children of your Father in Heaven." (Mt 5,45) It is because of the power and efficacy of the Father's love and forgiveness that the Christian is not only freed from sin but is welcomed into his Father's home. There he is a son who partakes of the joy, the peace, and the blessedness which the Father bestows in the kingdom of his only-begotten Son.

This kingdom is the central point of the message of the synoptic gospels. In them the Father is seen as establishing his reign "on earth as it is in heaven." (Mt 6,10) The petition of the Our Father in which we ask for the establishment of the kingdom shows the active, dynamic character of God's rule. It is established in Christ, but is meant to be spread to the hearts of all men in all ages. This kingdom is that "of the Father," "of God," or "of heaven"—for all three expressions mean essentially the actual sovereignty and ruling of God. The three phrases proclaim the kingship of the Father. This kingdom or reign is not

2

[1] A period between verse numbers indicates that the verses cited are successive but nonconsecutive.

primarily one in heaven but is something established here on earth by Christ.

The Individual's Relationship to Christ

Membership in the kingdom is determined by the relationship of the individual to Christ. "He who would save his life will lose it; but he who loses his life for *my* sake and for the sake of the gospel will save it." (Mk 8,35) Even if we must await the second coming of Christ for the glorious manifestation of this kingdom, the decisive age has arrived in this life; the Church is the present organ of the Father's glorious rule. Her life, the life of faith and grace, is hidden, though it contains the seeds of glory.

It is God acting in Christ who has established this kingdom. Man entering the kingdom must always be aware of this primacy of the divine initiative. Even when we have acted well and labored in the Lord's vineyard, we remain "unprofitable servants" (Lk 17,10) who must confess the power of the Father's love and the utter worthlessness of our activity separated from that love. This does not mean that the members of the kingdom are incapable of life and action but that a new life and activity enables them to share in Christ's work of establishing his kingdom. Only then can they achieve the destiny of being fully sons of the heavenly Father.

The Individual's Relationship to the Father

In preaching the kingdom, Jesus makes clear that the basic reality underlying it is God's fatherhood. The frequent designation of God as Father (cf. Mt 5,16.45.48; 6,1.4.6.8f.14f; 7,11.21, etc.) is a way of presenting to us the secret of God's action toward us in the order of salvation: *God is a Father who wishes us to become by grace his sons.*

The Old Testament had already spoken of God as loving Father, of Yahweh acting with love and mercy toward his people. When Jesus comes he presents his doctrine and himself as the fulfillment of the religion of the Old Testament. (Mt 5,17) The frequent use of the word *Father* to designate God who establishes his kingdom indicates that the distinctive relationship to God will be that of filial devotion.

What precisely is this relation of the Father to man, and how is man to enter into the relationship of sonship with God? God is the Father of all men, but there is a sense in which men must *become*, must change into sons. To accomplish this change they are invited to enter

3

into the kingdom. (Mt 5,45) The children of God (Mt 5,9.45; Lk 6,35), or the "children of the kingdom" (Mt 8,12), have *become* what they are, for not all men are inheritors of the kingdom. Although God is the Father of all, not all have answered his call to the kingdom. The members of the kingdom have received God's distinctive vocation and have responded by fidelity in a childlike disposition. They have thereby obtained the newness of life as sons. Only those who have been called to be sons and who have renounced the obstacle of sin can enter into this kingdom of grace. The quality of son pertains first and in a unique way to Christ, the beloved Son. Through him it is extended to the members of the kingdom in a real process of filiation and adoption.

A New Life and Faith

To receive Christ is to receive the kingdom, and this involves a certain inner disposition of heart. Man's receiving of the kingdom means welcoming a person, Christ (Mk 9,37), as well as receiving a message (Lk 8,13), the gospel of grace. The kingdom itself *is* grace as it establishes itself in the world and in the hearts of men. Grace is a transcendent good; it comes from God the Father by his gratuitous favor; it leads man to the loving and generous God of revelation. The effect of grace is to assure to man all that can fulfill him: salvation and beatitude. The grace of life in the kingdom is none other than the gift of salvation.

It is also beatitude, that is to say, a state in which man receives the pardon of his sins (Mt 6,14), the satisfaction of all his spiritual needs and of his most unlimited hopes. (Mt 25,34)

This grace is as interior and spiritual as the kingdom; it bestows a new principle of holiness and submission to God's will: the "justice" of the kingdom. (Mt 6,33) "The kingdom of God is within you" (Lk 17,21), but it is not completely invisible. The new principle of life in the kingdom must be at work giving expression of itself in good deeds, so that grace and the kingdom are as a leaven transforming the life of man even in this world. (Mt 13,33; Lk 13,20f) The inner reality of grace and the kingdom is thus incorporated into the external and visible organization of the Church, a society which has the spiritual goods of grace at its disposition. The life of grace is never a purely internal or purely individual reality. It is by its very structure the grace and kingdom of Christ established in this world on the foundation of the apostles. Jesus speaks of this kingdom as already established (Mt 12,28;

4

Lk 11,20), as present (Mt 11,12f; cf. Lk 16,16), and yet as still to be realized in its fullness in the future. (Cf. Lk 11,2; 19,11.) The kingdom begins with Jesus. To its establishment, all his work is directed.

In another sense the kingdom is, in its intellectual dimension, the living word or doctrine of Christ the divine Word, and thus it is the gospel that is the kingdom. (Mt 24,14) Put another way, the kingdom is likened to the seed of divine teaching. (Mt 13,19) Jesus speaks of the divine truths or mysteries which this kingdom comprehends. (Cf. Mt 13,11; Lk 8,10.)

This doctrine—the kingdom which is the gospel—is received in faith. Those who profess this faith are united in a single society which is the Church, the Israel of God founded on Peter. (Mt 16,19) Into this kingdom all men are invited with divine insistence (Mt 22,2–10), even to the eleventh hour. (Mt 20,1–16) The same recompense of grace is offered to all who answer the call of Christ. The kingdom is at once personal and social. Each man must enter it on his own account and live a personal life of justice, seeking at the same time that holy community which is the kingdom of God. (Mt 6,33; Lk 12,31)

God gives the aid of his grace to those who have been given the first grace of entrance into the kingdom. (Lk 12,32; Mt 13,11) The kingdom is thus a totally gratuitous gift; it is also a task or burden to be carried. This task is man's free cooperation with grace which always has the initiative. All the works, the good deeds, and activities of the kingdom are from God (cf. Mt 19,11); cooperation with his grace brings the reward of new graces. (Cf. Mk 4,24f; Mt 13,12; Lk 8,18; Mt 25,29.)

In Jesus and through him, therefore, is established the new and eternal rule of God which is a new covenant of the Father with the men who become brothers of Christ and truly sons of God. The whole purpose of the establishment of the kingdom is to institute a new order of salvation. The Father expresses his gracious love by providing a way of uniting men freely to himself. The kingdom is the symbolic reality of that grace which is bestowed on those who enter the kingdom but will come to perfection only in heaven. The kingdom is God uniting to himself, by a bond of love which is mutual, free, and ultimately eternal, the sinful human creature. Or, in more detail: "The kingdom is the society of men who, in Jesus Christ, possess the divine sonship, which is conserved and developed by struggle on this earth thanks to the mediation of their Savior, and which is perfectly developed and triumphant in heaven by a complete assimilation to their Savior." (J. Bonsirven, *Théologie du Nouveau Testament*, p. 64)

5

Receiving the Kingdom

The reception of grace means first of all the repentance always demanded by Christ (Mt 4,17; Mk 1,15; Lk 5,32; Lk 3,3.5; 24,47), that is, a renouncement of sin, a turning away from evil, a regret for past faults. But the reception of grace is also a movement to a new life, to Jesus, in fact, accomplished in faith. Faith in turn is the acceptance of his witness, the assent to his doctrine, and the acknowledgment of Jesus as the Christ; through him there is acceptance of the Father. (Cf. Mk 1,15; 11,31; Mt 18,6.) "He who believes and is baptized shall be saved, but he who does not believe shall be condemned." (Mk 16,16)

Faith is belief in God through Christ with an absolute sureness. Faith frees from sin. (Mk 2,5; Lk 7,50) Those who refuse faith are condemned for their failure to cooperate with grace. (Mt 11,20–24; Lk 13,28–30) The specific result of this divine gift of faith is possession of the kingdom, an abundant and imperishable reward. (Mt 7,24; 13,43) This faith comes from God (Mt 16,17) and is given only to those who are properly disposed (the "little ones" in Mt 11,25f; those around Christ in Mk 4,11.23.25 and Lk 8,10.) It is an assent to the gospel as well as to the power of Christ. Through faith man can see the testimony the Father renders to the Son. (Mt 11,2; Lk 7,18) By faith and baptism man enters into the kingdom.

The kingdom mentioned by the synoptic authors is a reality always associated with the inner transformation of grace. It is the infusion of a new life into the Christian, a fulfillment of the prophecies of a "new heart" and a "new spirit" in the Old Testament. (Ez 11,19; 36,25–27; Jer 31,31–34) Before this transformation man is spiritually lost and dead, but now like the prodigal son he is found again and is revivified: "because this my son was dead, and has come to life again; was lost and is found." (Lk 15,24.32) A new life is given by God. The justified man, like a good tree, bears new fruit (Mt 7,17), since he has become a "son of the kingdom" who has received the "good seed" sown by the "Son of Man." (Mt 13,38) He is become a child of the Father in heaven. (Mt 5,45) Because of this new life the members of the kingdom are to imitate the Father (Mt 5,48) as the model of their new life. Grace is to grow by a process of constant development and assimilation, that is, likeness to God himself.

The life of the kingdom is *life* in its fullest sense, in opposition to a way which leads to perdition. (Mt 7,13f) To possess this life is worth any sacrifice: "It is better for you to enter into life with one eye, than, having two eyes, to be cast into hell-fire." (Mt 18,9) Those who possess the kingdom shall enter into eternal life prepared for them in heaven: "Come, blessed of my Father, take possession of the kingdom prepared for you from the foundation of the world." (Mt 25,34) This is the destiny of grace. Thus the grace of the kingdom contains, as in a seed, the glory to come. The final glory of heaven is the crowning of the life of grace already initiated in the life of the kingdom in this world.

Conclusion

Man, created in the image of God (Gn 1,27), has that image restored in the reality of the coming of the kingdom: that is to say, the true destiny to which God intended man has been fully given back to him in the establishment of the kingdom described by the synoptics. The heart of their message is that the kingdom is here and now present and established in *Christ,* who has come to fulfill the expectations of the people Israel and to inaugurate the definitive period in the whole history of salvation. "The kingdom of God is at hand" (Mk 1,15), is the proclamation of the good tidings. It is established in the person and the works of Christ. (Lk 17,21)

In the recounting of the ministry of our Lord, the synoptics record the events of the power of God present in the founding of the kingdom and in the establishment of the Church. Small and humble as the Church may have been in its beginnings, it is, nevertheless, the manifestation of divine power and force, and its establishment presents each man with a challenge. Christ did not come merely to preach a new code of behavior, nor merely to reassert a proper conception of the true God: he came to found that kingdom through which salvation would be definitively offered to all men.

Entrance into the kingdom means more than a pledge of allegiance to Christ; it involves a more radical transformation than a merely external change of patterns of behavior. It does indeed involve new standards of judgment, higher ethical principles, and good works, all done in Christ's spirit. But it also means a new relationship with God: it means truly becoming sons of the Father in union with Christ. The Church has always understood this as signifying more than just an assent to a doctrine of the fatherhood of God and the brotherhood of men in Christ. For her it means a radical transformation of man from within. The kingdom is established socially in the Church, but it is also established individually within the depths of the being of each man who accepts the loving invitation of the Father. Becoming in a new and radical way a son of

7

God is not merely a matter of acknowledging God's dominion and mercy. It is truly to become a member of his family, to enter into a personal relation with him, to be reborn in faith and baptism into a new life. The life of grace is consistently described in the synoptics with reference to the establishment of Christ's kingdom on earth. Entrance into the kingdom is reception of a new and vital principle, really a new life, which comes to man as the result of the definitive conquering of sin by the death and resurrection of Christ.

SAINT JOHN

The New Life

The profoundly theological reflections of St. John present the reality of the kingdom of grace primarily under the symbol of a divine life communicated by the Father in Christ: "Yes, God has so loved the world that he has given his only Son that every man who believes in him may not perish but have eternal life." (Jn 3,16) Indeed, this is the purpose for which Christ himself entered the world: "I came that they may have life, and have it more abundantly." (Jn 10,10) The theme of life is the most prominent one in John's thought about Christ and his work. It is in terms of John's teaching on life in Christ and Christ's life in the individual Christian that his doctrine on grace will be developed.

First of all, Christ the Word is himself life: "In him was life, and the life was the light of men; the light shines in the darkness. . . . It was the true light that enlightens every man. . . . And the Word was made flesh, and dwelt among us. And we saw his glory . . . glory as of the only-begotten of the Father . . . full of *grace* and truth. . . . For the Law was given through Moses: *grace* and truth come through Jesus Christ." (Jn 1,4–17) The Word who has been made flesh bestows grace: "But to as many as received him he gave the power of becoming sons of God; to those who believe in his name: who were born not of blood, nor of the will of the flesh, nor of the will of man, but of God." (Jn 1,12f) Thus faith in the Word is the means by which man may open himself to the divine influence of grace and may become truly a son of God; like Christ (Jn 1,13; cf. *Bible de Jérusalem*), the Christian is born of God. (1 Jn 5,18) He who receives Christ in faith is born of God, and becomes the son of God by grace.

In the imagery of the fourth gospel, God himself is life: "For as the Father has life in himself. . . ." (Jn 5,26); in pouring out his love, he sends the Word who is himself life: "For as the Father has life in him-

8

self, even so he has given to the Son also to have life in himself." (*Ibid.*)
Through the Word men have the power to become sons of God. The
Word communicates "of his fullness" so that we may receive the "grace
and truth" that "come through Jesus Christ." (Jn 1,16f) Thus does
John trace the great lines of his vision of the divine plan for man's
salvation. God the Father who is love is the source and first principle of salvation. This divine love is manifested in the Word who
is light and life, and the Word "became flesh" and entered the world
in order to communicate to men the richness of grace, to bestow on man
life and light, rescuing man from death and darkness. Thus does John
summarize the essentials of the theology of grace: its source is the
divine life itself, in the love and life of the Father and of the eternal
Son; its realization comes in the course of human history by the incarnation of the Word of life, through whom we participate in the divine life
itself.

Christ: the New Life

Christ himself is a gift of grace, indeed *the* gift of grace, so that
Jesus says to the Samaritan woman: "If you but knew the gift of
God. . . ." (Jn 4,10) So too is he the life of God communicated to
man: "For as the Father raises the dead and gives them life, even so the
Son also gives life to whom he will." (Jn 5,21) The Father thus communicates his life, light, grace, and truth through the mediation of his
only-begotten Son, who is the mediator of all truth (Jn 8,31f) and of
all life: "For this is the will of my Father who sent me, that whoever
beholds the Son, and believes in him, shall have everlasting life, and I
will raise him up on the last day." (Jn 6,40)

John's profound realization of grace leads him to express over and
over again the fundamental religious conception of the Christian life
of grace as a full personal acknowledgment of the Word made flesh. To
those who receive Jesus, life is given. The life consists in knowing and
loving Christ and the brethren. "This is eternal life, that they may
know you, the only true God, and him who you have sent, Jesus Christ."
(Jn 17,3) To come to this life, sin must first be destroyed by the power
of "the lamb of God, who takes away the sins of the world." (Jn 1,29)

Sin is an enslavement to the world, seen as a principle of evil. It is
Christ who liberates man from this evil. "Amen, amen, I say to you,
everyone who commits sin is a slave of sin. But the slave does not abide
in the house forever; the son abides there forever. If therefore the son
makes you free, you will be free indeed." (Jn 8,34–37) It is not only St.

9

Paul, therefore, who draws a dramatic contrast between sin and justification, evil and grace. This conflict is presented clearly in St. John. Man's sin is destroyed by the Word: "To this end the Son of God appeared, that he might destroy the works of the devil. . . . and you know that he appeared to take our sins away, and sin is not in him." (1 Jn 3,8.5) It is the saving death of Christ that frees us: "And the blood of Jesus Christ, his Son, cleanses us from all sin." (1 Jn 1,7) Indeed, this work of grace and of new life is so powerful that the very principle of sin in man is destroyed, so that the Christian is not subject to sin so long as he remains in the life and grace of Christ: "Whoever is born of God does not commit sin, because his seed [the divine seed of the life of grace] abides in him and he cannot sin, because he is born of God." (1 Jn 3,9) "We know that no one who is born of God commits sin; but the Begotten of God preserves him and the evil one does not touch him." (1 Jn 5,18)

John does not deny that man can lose grace by his weakness, pride, and sinfulness. He does affirm in a positive strain that grace is a new life so powerful in and of itself that it gives man the power to resist sin, and thus to remain in the light. The Christian is, in principle, free of sin. Sin no longer has power over him. Man is still able to refuse the power of life and to succumb to death and evil, but this is not possible for the Christian who maintains his love for the Word who destroys sin.

New Birth in Christ

The destruction of the power of the evil one in the life of the Christian is accomplished by a new birth. John stresses above all else the positive aspects of grace by which we are reborn to a life of light, truth, and love. From the first chapter of his gospel, John affirms that Christ "gave the power of becoming sons of God: to those who believe in his name." (Jn 1,12) He emphasizes that this is not a mere figure of speech but a realistic description of a living, spiritual entity: "Behold what manner of love the Father has bestowed upon us, that we should be called children of God: *and such we are.*" (1 Jn 3,1)

This is a new birth "of water and the Spirit" (Jn 3,3.5) by which man is born again just as really as he was born by physical generation. This *re*-birth is a birth from on high, for the meaning of *again* in John's Greek vocabulary is "from on high" (Jn 3,3), that is, in the power of the Spirit. Man shares in the life of God by becoming a son of God: "That which is born of the Spirit is spirit." (Jn 3,6) This doctrine of a new creation is taken up again in forceful style by St. Paul, who stresses the redemptive aspect of this dramatic transformation of man.

10

John divides mankind into the children of God (Jn 11,52) and children of the devil (Jn 8,44); those who are "of God" (Jn 6,46; 1 Jn 3,10) and "of the truth" (1 Jn 3,19), and those who are "of the world" (Jn 8,23; 1 Jn 4,5) or "of the devil." (1 Jn 3,8) The whole first epistle is but an extended commentary on this spiritual reality. The letter should be studied in its entirety in light of the realism and dynamic forcefulness of John's conception of the communication to man of divine life. The same doctrine of the life "from on high" is developed in the third chapter of John's gospel in the discourse with Nicodemus (3,1–15), where the typical antithetical expressions of life and death, from on high and from below, from heaven and from the earth, occur. This passage also indicates that what the synoptics treated as the kingdom of God established in Christ is seen by John primarily in terms of a new life communicated through Christ:

vv. 1–11:   Christ asserts the necessity of a "birth from on high," that is, a birth in Christ who comes "from on high" and a birth befitting those who are to enter the kingdom of heaven, the kingdom "from on high." In this passage John goes beyond the expression of Mt 18,3, "Amen I say unto you, unless you turn and become like little children, you will not enter into the kingdom of heaven." Here one is not only to become "like" a child, one is to be born anew: not "of blood, nor of the will of the flesh, nor of the will of man" (Jn 1,13), but of God and of his Spirit. Nicodemus asks how this is possible. Christ replies: "By water and the Spirit." He then goes on to explain that by the action of the Spirit the man of flesh, of the world, is transferred into a new world and is "of the Spirit." A divine force is bestowed on him by the Spirit, a new generation. This action of the Spirit is as invisible as that of the wind (and John here plays on the double sense of the Greek word *pneuma* for wind and spirit.) Thus is evoked the Old Testament description in Gn 2,7 where Yahweh breathes life into man. The breath, the spirit, is an Old Testament figure of divine action (cf. Job 34,14f; Ex 15,8); John recalls too the "new spirit" promised in Ezechiel. (Ez 36,26f) Jesus thus can reproach Nicodemus for his lack of spiritual understanding of the power and efficacy of God's Spirit. In these verses the affirmations of Christ are met by lack of understanding on the part of Nicodemus, but Christ takes up the conversation again by turning attention to "heavenly things."

vv. 12–15:   "If I have spoken of earthly things to you, and you do not believe, how will you believe if I speak to you of heavenly things? No one has ascended into heaven except him who has descended from   *11* heaven: the Son of Man who is in heaven. And as Moses lifted up the serpent in the desert, even so must the Son of Man be lifted up, that those who believe in him may not perish, but may have life everlasting." What are these "heavenly things"? Verse 13 probably refers to the ascension of Christ which manifests that he who descended from heaven is he who always was in heaven. (Cf. Phil 2,6–10.) The reality, as well as the full understanding of the reality of the new birth, depends on the glorified Christ and on the Spirit whom he sends. (Jn 7,39) Jesus points to himself as the source of understanding of the doctrine he enunciates to Nicodemus. In vv. 12–15 he directs attention not to the Old Testament allusion of vv. 1–11, but to himself and to his future glorification. He is therefore referring to the elevation of the bronze serpent in the desert as a symbol of his crucifixion and glorious ascension.

In this passage John teaches that entrance into the kingdom is reserved for those who are born again. This is possible only in the Spirit from "on high"; the coming of this Spirit is the result of the death and glorification of Christ. We can see a complementary doctrine in St. Paul: "He saved us through the bath of regeneration and renewal by the Holy Spirit; whom he has abundantly poured out upon us through Jesus Christ our Savior, in order that, justified by his grace, we may be heirs in the hope of life everlasting." (Ti 3,5f) This brings out clearly the allusion in John to "water and the Spirit," that is to baptism, the sacrament of rebirth in which the Spirit renews man. The Spirit was given to Christ at his baptism through John the Baptist in order that the faithful might in turn receive him. (Jn 1,29–34) Grace and the Spirit come to man in a sacramental rite in baptism; this rite is received, as the text indicates, in faith. The remainder of this part of the chapter (vv. 16–21) emphasizes the consequences of the new birth, and stresses the fact that this birth into the life of grace, normally bestowed in baptism, is but the beginning of a new way of living.

The True Light

If the reality of grace is presented in John in terms of the great symbol of life, it is also a part of the Johannine symbolism to see Christ as the light, the true light (Jn 1,9), the light of the world. (Jn 8,12; 9,5) Grace is an illumination making of Christians "children of light." (Jn 12,36; cf. Lk 16,8.) The whole episode of Chapter 9 on the curing of the man born blind may be read as an instruction on the marvelous effects of Christ, the light, restoring the vision and the apprehension of spiritual realities to man. God himself is light. (1 Jn 1,5) He is the eternal truth opposed to darkness and error. John sees light and life as interchangeable concepts in speaking of the Word. (Jn 1,3f) Those who receive the light have the knowledge of God which makes them sons of God and partakers of his life. Those who receive the light become sharers in the true light that God himself is from all eternity.

The reception of this light by man is the beginning of a process of progressive illumination effected in the Christian by his cooperation with the "Spirit of truth" (Jn 14,17; 15,26) who will teach you "all truth." (Jn 16,13) The life of grace is a "coming to the light" (Jn 3,21) and a form of existence "in the light." (Cf.1 Jn 2,8f.) In John, then, the designation of God or the Word as light and as truth is not a mere indication that Christ is the source or even the object of "true doctrine." It is much more, for light and truth designate the fullness of reality, the plenitude of being which God is and which is manifested to man in Christ.

Thus, too, the fact that Christians, having been enlightened by Christ, accept his truth, means more than that they give assent to the truth about Jesus. It means an access to new being, an entrance into divine being itself, to such an extent that the Christian is a "son of the light." He receives a new mode of existence in the light, as a partaker of the life which is light. If this great symbol of light in John has an intellectual dimension—so that the life of grace is defined in terms of a knowledge of the Father and the Son (Jn 17,3)—we must see in the Johannine doctrine of light a profound reality which sees the light as God himself. Our participation in this light is thus another way used by John to reveal the mystery of the Christian's sharing in the ultimate reality which God is, by way of a decisive regeneration. This rebirth separates him from sin and darkness. It introduces man into the life of God who is light and truth.

John explains the mystery of the kingdom described in the synoptics in terms which are distinctively his own: by the use of the great antithetic pairs of symbols, death and life, darkness and light. The notion of eternal life was of course present in the synoptics: "What good work shall I do to have eternal life? . . . If you will enter into life, keep the commandments." (Mt 19,16f; cf. Mk 9,43.45.) Or again: "And these will go into everlasting punishment, but the just into everlasting life," which is the "kingdom prepared for you from the foundation of the world." (Mt 25,46.34) However, it is only in John that the reality of life is treated so thoroughly and with such depth. What was implicit in the synoptics becomes the core of John's profound theological meditations.

Grace and Glory

We have seen in the synoptics the doctrine of the kingdom presented in its two distinct phases: that of establishment and beginning on earth in this life, and that of completion and fulfillment in the next life at the last judgment. John does not deny or even overlook this distinction between the life of grace and the life of glory. "He who loves his life, loses it; and he who hates his life in this world, keeps it unto life everlasting." (Jn 12,25) In the discourse at the last supper, Christ explains to the disciples: "In my Father's house there are many mansions. Were it not so, I should have told you, because I go to prepare a place for you. And if I go and prepare a place for you, I am coming again, and I will take you to myself; that where I am, there you may also be." (Jn 14,2f) More often, however, John sees the whole Christian life as a unity, and stresses the mystery that eternal life is already present, has already begun, here on earth. In a sense, then, John sees the last days as already accomplished in what has been called his "realized eschatology." That is to say, John sees the essentials of life in God and union with the Word as a realization here and now of the glory to come. The life of grace is a real anticipation of the life of heaven.

John expresses the positive aspect of our transformation into a state of sharing in the life of God as something already essentially accomplished, without denying that this new life is yet to come in its full perfection. The believer already possesses eternal life: "Amen, amen, I say to you, he who hears my word, and believes him who sent me, has life everlasting, and does not come to judgment, but has passed from death to life" (Jn 5,24); and: "He who believes in the Son has everlasting life." (Jn 3,15.36; cf. 6,47; 1 Jn 5,11–13.) This is affirmed too in the Johannine chapter on the eucharist in connection with the effects of this sacrament: "He who eats my flesh and drinks my blood has life everlasting and I will raise him up on the last day." (Jn 6,55) The realism of these statements indicates that John is not speaking about the believer in the last days. Rather he inculcates the notion of the present reality of the divine life within man, which transforms him into a son of God.

The third chapter of the first epistle expresses the conviction that the divine life is now present as a result of the new generation by God:

14   v. 1:   "Behold what manner of love the Father has bestowed upon us, that we should be called children of God: and such we are."

This is a strong affirmation of the present reality of our divine rebirth. It is a favorite theme of John, one that will be affirmed also by St. Paul. This whole inner realism of grace will be one of the major affirmations of Catholic teaching through the ages. We see its foundation clearly in apostolic teaching.

v. 2: "Beloved, now we are children of God, and it has not yet appeared what we shall be. We know that, when he appears, we shall be like to him, for we shall see him just as he is." John here notes the fact that our present state of sonship is to be perfected and consummated in glory—a state which we do not yet know or see. But the consummation of this life of grace in what is called the beatific vision of God is rooted in the present real state of transformation. Glory is but the further perfection of it. The reality of the transformation of grace is an indication and assurance of the future glorification of the sons of God.

v. 9: "Whoever is born of God does not commit sin, because his seed abides in him. . . ." This text, in the usual exegesis, sees the "seed" of God in us as the internal principle of divine life, and thus is another affirmation of the inner reality of grace. The verse may also be rendered, "because his lineage remains in him"—this either in a collective sense: that we are of the race of God; or in an individual sense: that Christ remains in us. (Cf. Gal 3,16.) In either reading, the strong reality of the present state of the Christian is proposed.

vv. 10f.14: ". . . Whoever is not just is not of God, nor is he just who does not love his brother. For this is the message that you have heard from the beginning, that we should love one another. . . . We know that we have passed from death to life, because we love the brethren." The great sign which is the natural and necessary manifestation of the reality of the divine life in us is that this new life is expressed in good works of justice, all of which John summarizes in "the love of the brethren." This is the necessary mark of him who has passed into the life of Christ: "By this will all men know that you are my disciples, if you have love for one another." (Jn 13,35) Again in this chapter we read: "Everyone who hates his brother is a murderer. And you know that no murderer has eternal life abiding in him." (v. 15) The whole passage insists on the difference between those who possess life, who are living, and the sons of the world or of Satan who do not possess this life and cannot manifest its sign which is fraternal love. There is then a *15* real inner transformation that makes the Christian a son of the Father who, in all that he does, manifests this inner life. The life of grace is a force leading to a mode of activity proper to it. We may say that John sees the total Christian reality as a process which has its beginning and its progressive unfolding in love, and its consummation in glory. There, our sonship will be fully manifest in the vision of God.

Life in God

The complete reality of the inner transformation of the life of grace is brought out by St. John in his repeated mention of the new presence to the Christian of the Father and Son: that is, the real indwelling presence of the persons of the Trinity. "He who confesses the Son has the Father also. As for you, let that which you have heard from the beginning abide in you. If that abides in you which you have heard from the beginning, you also will abide in the Son and in the Father. And this is the promise he has given us, the life everlasting." (1 Jn 2,23–25) This eternal life, which is now present to us, is not only a change within the Christian but is also the actual presence of the Father and Son in us. John writes of the Son: "This is the testimony, that God has given us eternal life; and this life is in his Son. He who has the Son has the life. He who has not the Son has not the life." (1 Jn 5,11f) Not only is the Christian given life, which later theology will call created habitual grace, but he is given "uncreated grace": the actual presence of the persons of the Trinity.

It is this life in the presence of the Son which will be consummated in glory but which is now hidden in faith. "I am the resurrection and the life; he who believes in me, even if he die, shall live; and whoever lives and believes in me, shall never die." (Jn 11,25f) The principle of deathless life is already communicated to the Christian who lives in Christ. The physical reality of this mutual presence of the Christian and Christ is placed in a strong light by the parable of the vine and the branches: "Abide in me, and I in you. As the branch cannot bear fruit of itself unless it remains on the vine, so neither can you unless you abide in me. I am the vine, you are the branches. He who abides in me, and I in him, bears much fruit. . . ." (Jn 15,4f) The whole parable teaches that the life which Christ is, is transmitted to us, the branches, so that there is a communion in the same life. This vital and intimate connection involves *a mutual presence of man to Christ and Christ to man* which is the constant condition of the life of the Christian. This life furthermore fructifies and expresses its dynamic nature by the good works which manifest the life of the branches in vital communion with the vine. Indeed, one text in this parable: "without me you can do nothing," will be constantly present to the theological awareness of the Church in her doctrinal development.

"In that day you will know that I am in my Father, and you in me, and I in you." (Jn 14,20) Here the union of the Father and Son within the absolute unity of the godhead is made the principle of the union of life which is established between Christ and the Christian. This is not a mere harmony of thoughts; it is more than a friendship. It is a real if mysterious dimension of the intimate relationship established through grace between Christ and him who has received Christ's life. The whole divine plan is here accomplished and summarized. In the Christian are "repeated" in a real way all the marvels of the inner life of the Trinity. The Father who is love is the unique source of the life (Jn 5,26) which is communicated from all eternity to the Word, who thus "has [or is] life in himself." (Jn 5,26; cf. 1,13.) The "becoming flesh," the incarnation, of the Word is the manifestation to man of the life which the Son has from the Father: "And the Life was made known and we have seen, and now testify and announce to you, the life eternal which was with the Father, and has appeared to you." (1 Jn 1,2)

The whole meaning of this manifestation of the love of the Father is to communicate life to man. (Jn 3,16; 10,10) All men may receive this life if they are not so attached to sin and darkness as to refuse the light. For those who receive this life there is entrance into communion with the divine persons, a sharing by grace in the life which is proper to God alone. This union with Christ perfects the union among those men who are joined in fraternal charity. The union which binds Christians together is an imitation of the unity which unites Father, Son, and Spirit, and the result of the wonderful presence to the Christian of the Father and Son: "If anyone love me, he will keep my word, and my Father will love him, and we will come and make our abode with him." (Jn 14,23) In these words John seeks to express the inexpressible mystery of shared life which incorporates man into the divine life of the Trinity.

This incorporation is at once individual and personal as well as social. As the parable of the vine and the branches indicates, our union with Christ is also a union in the reality of the one life of the Church. This union which the Christian expresses by keeping the commandments, and above all by loving the brethren, unites him in a profound union with his fellow Christian. The ecclesial aspect of grace is thus one of the aspects of the divine life in man which John clearly teaches.

Conclusion

The divine life originates in the Father and is communicated to the eternal Word. From Father and Son proceeds the Holy Spirit, who is, as it were, the perfecting of the inner life of God. It is through and in the Spirit that we enter into the life of God. Through his efficacious divine power we become sons in the Son and are united in the Spirit, through Christ, to the Father. St. John presents us with a profound revelation of the doctrine of grace: the result of his penetration, in the Spirit, into the mysteries of our relationship with the triune God. The Christian thus becomes a son of God, a child of truth and light, by a communication of divine life and truth which transfers him from the world of sin and darkness into the glorious kingdom of God. This communication of divine life, effected in the rebirth of baptism through faith and constantly renewed in the eucharist, is a real beginning here on earth of the life of glory to come. This life of glory will be but the flowering and the open manifestation of the inner transformation which has already taken place in the life of grace.

SAINT PAUL

The rich and varied thought of St. Paul is difficult to summarize, for his letters were not written as systematic works. His teaching on any one topic is to be found in many different places under various aspects. Nevertheless, no treatment of grace and redemption would be adequate without an examination of the main lines of Pauline theology, which has exerted so strong an influence on all later religious thought about Christ and his work. As is his custom, Paul develops the less complex thought of the synoptics to suit his purposes of exposition, argument, or exhortation. He presents his reflections on the central Christian mysteries with an abundance and profusion which contrasts with and complements the thought of St. John.

There are numerous and original differences distinguishing the thought of St. Paul, although whenever the writers express Christian realities in their characteristic thought patterns the profound unity of New Testament thought is preserved. St. Paul surely expresses a fundamental New Testament theme when he sees the purpose of God's creation as making all men his children by uniting them to his Son, Jesus Christ, as brothers. "He predestined us to be adopted through Jesus Christ as his sons, according to the purpose of his will, unto the praise of the glory of his grace, with which he had favored us in his beloved Son." (Eph 1,5f)

The process of assuming man into the life of God involves first the negative aspect of freeing man from all that separates him from God and holiness, then the positive aspect of incorporating man into Christ through the Spirit so that he may live for the Father. These two elements, while inseparable in Paul's thought, are dramatically distinguished in the description of the work of redemption.

Christ and Salvation

The divine plan of the salvation of man is accomplished in the work of Christ; he thus becomes the center of the whole reality of mankind and human destiny. The connection between the work of redemption, through the coming of Christ and his death and glorious resurrection, and the reality of Christ as occupying the first and central role in God's actual creation, is expressed in this magnificent passage:

> He [the Father] has rescued us from the power of darkness and transferred us into the kingdom of his beloved Son, in whom we have our redemption, the remission of our sins. He is the image of the invisible God, the firstborn of every creature. For in him were created all things in the heaven and on earth, things visible and things invisible, whether Thrones, or Dominations, or Principalities, or Powers. All things have been created through and unto him, and he is before all creatures, and in him all things hold together. (Col 1,13–17)

The reality of Christ appears thus as the climax of all creation, as the goal of God's action from eternity. The coming of Christ, and the subsequent elevation of the faithful man into Christ and his life, does not appear, in the light of this text, as a divine afterthought to the creation of the universe. By his incarnation the divine Word of John's gospel is the real consummation of the whole of creation. The historical event of Christ's coming means that God has assumed into himself the very fabric of human history. In this sense the whole of the reality of creation and history centers in the incarnate person, Christ. Thus the whole religion of Christianity is "to re-establish all things in Christ, both those in the heavens and those on the earth." (Eph 1,10) God's communication of himself to man is realized not only in the creation of the world and of the human race, but primarily in him who is the firstborn of every creature, who communicates to us in grace his own life.

Grace for Paul: In God and in Man

It has been usual in the history of theology to speak of the difference between the Greek Fathers, who emphasized in the work of Christ the realization of the eternal divine will for the divinization of man, and the Western Fathers, notably St. Augustine, who stressed the historical reality of the redemptive purpose of the incarnation. It may be said that both these elements are found in St. Paul, and that it is well to see all aspects of the mystery of Christ if we are to understand what God has accomplished in him. *Through the incarnation Christ realizes to the full God's expression of himself to his creature by assuming humanity unto himself.* Thus, by bringing man into the divine life, God washes away the sins of man and bestows on him the life of grace. The word *salvation* may be used to signify this whole process, or better perhaps, the term *grace*.

Grace means both the loving benevolence of the Father manifested in Christ and the divine gifts bestowed on us in Christ by which we are saved, that is, sanctified in being made like to him. In the first sense, grace is a property or characteristic of God; rather it is God himself in his benevolence and love for man, willing man's salvation through the historical acts of Christ in the Spirit. "He predestined us to be adopted through Jesus Christ as his sons, according to the purpose of his will. . . . In him, I say, in whom we also have been called by a special choice, having been predestined in the purpose of him who works all things . . . to the praise of his glory. . . ." (Eph 1,5.11f) Grace is first the love of the Father by which he has chosen us in Christ; Paul therefore speaks of the grace that is God communicating grace to us:

> But God who is rich in mercy, by reason of his very great love wherein he has loved us even when we were dead by reason of our sins, brought us to life together with Christ (by grace you have been saved) . . . that he might show in the ages to come the overflowing riches of his gracious kindness towards us in Christ Jesus. (Eph 2,4–7)

Grace, then, is a word which can be applied both to the loving mercy of the Father and to those redemptive works of Christ which make God's love operative in the world. In this second sense grace applies to God and his saving deeds in Christ. The latter may be called redemption in the objective sense, referring, that is, to the reality of the Father's love manifested in the redemptive actions of Christ's passion and resurrection. Grace and redemption can thus refer to what happened in and through Christ; "the work of grace" can refer to the central reality of saving history: the redemptive actions of Christ. These actions may be called grace or graces, for they are in themselves the merciful, "gracious" effects of the totally gratuitous love of the Father for us. Since grace and redemption from this point of view have been discussed elsewhere in this series, we shall confine ourselves to grace within man.

The grace by which we are saved can refer to the supernatural realities of our transformation into Christ, that is, our "subjective" and personal assimilation of the saving effects of Christ's objective redemption. We shall deal with grace as something within man; it is, quite simply, the sanctification of man incorporated into Christ by faith and baptism. We thus consider not so much what has taken place in and through Christ as what happens, through Christ and in the Spirit, within man himself. This distinction will enable us to consider grace insofar as it refers to the realities of the process of our Christianization.

POSITIVE AND NEGATIVE ASPECTS OF GRACE   In order to try to comprehend the rich variety of Pauline thought, we shall examine passages from the epistles in a schematic rather than in a chronological way. This will be done in accordance with the understanding of man's sanctification as achieved in a twofold process: that of a freeing of man from all that separates him from God, and that of a positive incorporation into Christ. This distinction is, of course, only for the sake of order. The actual process is at one and the same time a liberation and a sanctification, a pardon and destruction of sin and a bestowal of grace and new life. Paul in fact sees both aspects together:

> He has rescued us from the power of darkness and transferred us into the kingdom of his beloved Son in whom we have our redemption, the remission of sins. . . . You yourselves were at one time estranged and enemies in mind through your evil works. But now he has reconciled you in his body of flesh through his death, to present you holy and undefiled and irreproachable before him. (Col 1,13f.21f)

Paul continually emphasizes that we are saved only in Christ and through his grace; moreover, he sees this salvation as effected first in a rescuing or liberation from sin and darkness, and then as the reconciliation or transfer of man into Christ. Catholic understanding has always seen in these Pauline expressions assertions of a real and radical transformation. The change takes place in man as the result of the bestowal upon him of the benefits of Christ's redemptive action. In other

21

words, our incorporation into Christ involves a real conversion from one state or condition of reality to a new one. An actual change is effected within man:

> For the grace of God our Savior has appeared to all men, instructing us that, rejecting ungodliness and worldly lusts, we may live temperately and justly and piously in this world; looking for the blessed hope and glorious coming of our great God and Savior, Jesus Christ, who gave himself for us that he might redeem us from all iniquity and cleanse for himself an acceptable people, pursuing good works. (Ti 2,11–14)

Liberation from Sin

Christ does not free us from what is good: from our natures, ourselves, or the world seen as coming from God. He frees us from sin, the barrier decisively separating us from God. Sin is seen by Paul not in some mere legal sense as a transgression of precept, but as a personal offense against God and his will, a revolt which leads, consequently, to death. Sin rules in the man who has not been freed by Christ: "All have sinned and have need of the glory of God." (Rom 3,23) The first three chapters of the epistle to the Romans are a description of the sinful state of the gentiles who did not have the Law of Moses, but the natural guidance of the law that is written in men's hearts; they also describe the Jews who transgressed the revealed Law given them on Sinai. Both have sinned by violating the moral law, which each knew in one way or another: "Tribulation and anguish shall be visited upon the soul of every man who works evil; of Jew first, and then of Greek. . . . For whoever have sinned without the Law, will perish without the Law; and whoever have sinned under the Law, will be judged by the Law." (Rom 2,9.12) The religious privileges of the Jews are indeed worthy of praise and respect (Rom 3,1–2), but by themselves they do not overcome sin nor are they able to prevent sin. The Jew is as much the sinner as the gentile who is without the Law. "What then? Are we [as Jews] better off than they? Not at all. For we have argued that Jews and Greeks are all under sin." (Rom 3,9)

It is not only the fact of universal sin that Paul recognizes, but sin in some way personified. Paul can speak of sin as ruling or governing: "As sin has reigned unto death, so also grace may reign by justice unto life everlasting through Jesus Christ our Lord." (Rom 5,21) Man is subjected to sin as to a master: "But thanks be to God that you who were slaves of sin have now obeyed from the heart that form of doctrine

22

into which you have been delivered." (Rom 6,17) This is not to say, of course, that man has no freedom, or that he is totally subject to the tyranny of sin; yet Paul sees sin as a power constantly working against man, taking advantage of his weakness, and producing death as its consequence: "Now the sting of sin is death, and the power of sin is the Law." (1 Cor 15,56)

The Law increases consciousness of sin, but by its very impotence to aid man in avoiding sin, it multiplies sin. In a sense it is used by sin to increase sin's dominion over man. St. Paul does not deny the responsibility of those who sin, but he affirms the sinful plight of man without Christ. Sin is often stronger than man and is able to dominate him, so that "sin abounds" without the saving and healing grace of Christ.

"You, when you were dead by reason of your sins and the uncircumcision of your flesh, he brought to life along with him, forgiving you all your sins, cancelling the decree against us, which was hostile to us. Indeed, he has taken it completely away, nailing it to the cross." (Col 2,13f) The sentence or decree of guilt which was the result of sin has been destroyed by the power of the redemptive act of Christ on the cross. "If then any man is in Christ, he is a new creature: the former things have passed away; behold they are made new. But all things are from God, who has reconciled us to himself through Christ. . . . For God was truly in Christ, reconciling the world to himself by not reckoning against men their sins. . . . We exhort you, for Christ's sake, be reconciled to God. For our sakes he made him to be sin who knew nothing of sin, so that in him we might become the justice of God." (2 Cor 5,17–21)

This text states the equivalence of being a Christian and being in Christ. The Christian becomes a "new creature"; God no longer imputes sin to man for he has remitted his sin. This is not a mere nonimputation of sin, as if God were to overlook the sin of man. The whole realistic tone of this passage indicates a genuine reconciliation with God which involves a real blotting out of sin, not merely a forgetting of it.

Liberation from the Flesh

Man is subject to the power of sin in part because of "the flesh," which is not, as such, the bodily nature of man but the source of weakness and evil in him, the principle of sin within man. We saw that Paul assumes (Rom 1–3) on man's part sufficient and basic knowledge of moral goodness. He sees man so weakened in the flesh, however, that he appears incapable of avoiding evil. According to Paul, sin reveals

23

itself in and through the sins of human persons. Sin takes over that which is good and uses the body as an instrument for evil: "Did then that which is good become death to me? By no means! But sin that it might be manifest as sin, worked death for me through that which is good. . . . For I know that in me, that is, in my flesh, no good dwells, because to wish is within my power, but I do not find the strength to accomplish what is good. . . . Therefore I myself with my mind serve the law of God, but with my flesh the law of sin." (Rom 7,13–25) The members of the body are capable of becoming instruments of sin: "And do not yield your members to sin as weapons of iniquity." (Rom 6,13)

By flesh, note, Paul does not mean primarily the body or the material principle which is part of man's created nature. He does not consider man philosophically, as a theoretician of the structure of man would do, but views him in a totally religious context. The "flesh" is not so much a part of man studied from the philosophical point of view in his body-soul composition; rather, "flesh" is seen in the context of an inner religious struggle in man which opposes the spirit to the flesh, the principle of good and of the knowledge of God to the principle of evil and of sin. Flesh, in Paul's understanding of the term, is man lacking both the power of God's saving grace and the Spirit of God who overcomes evil.

The famous passage in Romans 7 pictures man as divided against himself. In this context flesh is equivalent to the whole array of forces which oppose man to God and make him subject to sin. The desires of the flesh lead to evil and death: "But I say: walk in the Spirit, and you will not fulfill the lusts of the flesh. For the flesh lusts against the spirit, and the spirit against the flesh; for these are opposed to each other . . . and they who belong to Christ have crucified their flesh with its passions and desires." (Gal 5,16f.24)

The flesh is a source of evil, not identified with the body as such but with a principle of sinfulness which is the work of Satan. It is the result of the reign of sin initiated by the fall of Adam. Thus the works of the flesh are not only sexual or carnal sins, though St. Paul realizes the gravity and extent of such faults (Rom 1,26ff), but all sin. He attributes human proneness to sin to an evil inherent not only in the body but in man as such. In the pagans it leads to idolatry, basically a refusal to give God due service and honor: "They who exchanged the truth of God for a lie, and worshipped and served the creature rather than the Creator. . . . For this cause God has given them up to shameful lusts." (Rom 1,25f) Thus, among the works of the flesh in Romans 1 and Galatians 5 Paul enumerates sins which we might call spiritual sins:

24

envy, disobedience, pride, anger. *It is from the power of the sinful force of the flesh that the grace of Christ delivers men.*

When Paul speaks of the "sinful flesh" (Rom 8,3) and the "body of sin" (Rom 6,6) and sees the flesh as the instrument of sin within man, the reality of the religious struggle between good and evil becomes clear. It is Paul's attempt to make man aware of his unhappy state and to help him live in full reliance on the Spirit, who strengthens man's spirit by grace. Without grace "I am carnal (fleshly), sold into the power of sin." (Rom 7,14) Without the redemptive action of Christ communicated through the Spirit, man remains subject to the flesh, and through the flesh to sin. The new Adam who is Christ destroys the power of the flesh which was initiated when, by Adam's sin, all men became sinners. "Therefore as through one man sin entered into the world and through sin death, and thus death has passed unto all men because all have sinned. . . ." (Rom 5,12)

Since man is born of Adam into a race over which sin exercises a real power, St. Paul can say of man: "We were by nature children of wrath even as the rest." (Eph 2,3) It is only by grace that man is freed from sin. By being liberated in Christ, he is also free of the wrath of God. God's "wrath" we may take as the powerful expression, in Paul's vocabulary, of the enmity existing between the sinner and God. The phrase is a strong reminder of the fact that sin is an offense against the person of God. "For the wrath of God is revealed from heaven against all ungodliness and wickedness of those men who in wickedness hold back the truth of God. . . ." (Rom 1,18; cf. Rom 2,5; 9,22; Eph 5,6; 1 Thes 2,16.) But as has been pointed out, man is freed from sin, freed from the power of the flesh, and thus freed too from the wrath of God because of the redemptive acts of Christ shared in by man through grace. ". . . To serve the living and true God, and to await from heaven Jesus, his Son, whom he raised from the dead, who has delivered us from the wrath to come." (1 Thes 1,9f)

Liberation from the flesh and from its power to seduce man and lead him into sin, that is, into incurring yet more the just wrath of God, is thus a freeing which is negative. It is equally positive, for it transfers man from the power of sin to the power of grace in Christ. This is not merely the liberation from a state of evil into some neutral condition; it is the inner transformation of the sinner into Christ, so that his condition and his allegiance are no longer those of the flesh. This is a change which affects man in a very real and profound sense: it is not merely a humanly achieved self-control, nor the result of a new determination or enthusiasm. It is that which really changes man into Christ and frees

25

him from the power which the flesh, the sinful principle, has without grace.

Liberation from the Law

St. John made allusion to the decisive change in the divine work of man's salvation instituted by the crucial event of the Word's becoming flesh: "For the law was given through Moses; grace and truth come through Jesus Christ." (Jn 1,17) The whole order of the Old Testament is now not eliminated but fulfilled; it has come to the moment of its complete maturation in Christ—the appointed moment in which divine activity within the world reaches its climax. "But when the fullness of time came, God sent his Son, born of a woman, born under the Law, that he might redeem those who were under the Law, that we might receive the adoption of sons." (Gal 4,4f) The revelation of God in the Old Testament, the promises made to Abraham, the covenant with Moses, were all to be consummated in the incarnation of the Word as Christ. A new order of salvation, founded in the presence of Christ, would bring to its final stage that sacred history by which the life of man was taken into the life of God and the action of God entered into the action of man. *St. Paul sees this crowning action of history as a freeing of man from the Law:* "The Law of the commandments expressed in decrees he has made void." (Eph 2,15) "But now we have been set free from the Law." (Rom 7,6) The Law then was a provisional work of God's saving action among men, destined to be superseded by Christ. "What was the Law? It was enacted on account of transgressions, being delivered by angels through a mediator, until the offspring should come to whom the promise was made." (Gal 3,19) A new era has arrived; man has been freed from the Law and its binding character.

St. Paul goes beyond affirming the passing of the economy of the Law and the coming of Christ, seeing the liberation from the Law as a positive good associated with the kingdom of grace. In some way the Law was a sign, even an instrument, of the reign of sin: ". . . for sin shall not have dominion over you, since you are not under the Law but under grace." (Rom 6,14) Just as the flesh was a source of sin and a principle of evil residing within man, so in a way did the Law influence man's life. Much of Paul's thought on this matter develops in his opposition to those converts from Judaism who wished to retain the practices of the Jewish Law. Paul saw this Judaizing position as one which derogated from the perfection of the regime of Christ; therefore he

26

fought against those who would demand the following of the Law as a condition of salvation through Christ.

LAW AND SALVATION   What is the importance of this controversy for us? Has it merely an historical value, as giving insight into the struggles of the developing Christian community? No. This controversy of Paul's with the upholders of the Law goes deeper. It touches the heart of the Christian's relations with God. Paul is waging the same fundamental battle that Christ waged against the pharisees who put their confidence for salvation in strict adherence to the Law. Paul's argument is directed against all who seek salvation through legalistic observance of the letter of the Law.

There are those, then, who to a greater or lesser degree expect God's favor and salvation to come by and through their own external obedience. Paul condemns this attitude on two levels. That the purely external carrying out of the Law is valueless by itself is clear; let us suppose, however, that a man obeys the Law conscientiously and not in the self-satisfied, hypocritical manner of the pharisees. A man keeps the Law in his outward behavior as well as within, in his conscience and in his heart. Is this man saved by his obedience to the Law? St. Paul's answer is a vigorous denial, for he sees that salvation neither is nor ever can be the result of human effort, no matter how conscientious and lawful. Rather, salvation comes from God alone and from his grace by faith—also a gift of God. Good works and moral action come indeed from the gift of grace, but grace is the work of the Father through Christ in the Spirit, and is never produced by the good works or the obedience to law accomplished by human effort alone.

The Christian who lives in the truth must live above all by the truth of the primacy of God's grace. Grace, of course, does not save man without his free cooperation in faith and love, but it is through the power of grace that man's cooperation leads to salvation. Fundamentally, St. Paul is condemning not only those who, in his own day, sought salvation through obedience to the Jewish Law but also all those who would so seriously misunderstand Christianity as to make it a regime of law rather than one of the Spirit and of grace.

The argument may be carried further. It may be said that the Law alone is powerless to bring man into the life of God. The Law is an expression in imperative form of principles of moral good and evil. It is a guide, a determined rule of conduct, but it has no power of life within itself. St Paul points out the complete inadequacy of the Law in this

27

sense; he even sees the Law as multiplying sin. In itself it is good, for it comes from God: "The Law indeed is holy and the commandment holy and just and good." (Rom 7,12) The religious edifice of the Old Testament is the work of God in which Paul rejoices (Rom 3,2; 9,4), but the Law does not change man. Rather, it gives knowledge of the principles of good action but does not communicate the power to obey these divine commandments. "For the letter kills, but the Spirit gives life." (2 Cor 3,6)

LAW AND SIN   Paul goes on to explain this statement by saying that the regime of the Law was a "ministration of death." (2 Cor 3,7) The Law made clear each of the moral commandments and thus made sin not a mere failing but an action against God himself as revealed in his Law; that is to say, "through Law comes the recognition of sin." (Rom 3,20) A knowledge of the commandments of the Law was thus the occasion of a greater sinfulness on man's part; man was now a transgressor of commandments whose meaning and import he was aware of. In giving a greater knowledge of sin, the Law increased sin by increasing man's responsibility and awareness. It added to the gravity of sin by making evil-doing a transgression against the explicit will of God. Indeed, in a mysterious sentence, Paul says: "Now the Law intervened that the offense might abound." (Rom 5,20)

How then could the Law be called good when sin increased on the occasion of its promulgation? Paul's immediate answer is: "But where the offense has abounded, grace has abounded yet more." (Rom 5,20) In the providential order of God, the Law was a means of bringing man to a heightened consciousness of his own weakness. This awareness makes even more striking the new abundance of grace communicated to man in Christ. The point which Paul wishes to emphasize is again the primacy and transcendence of grace; the Law serves only as a means to awaken a profound sense of human weakness and of the need for divine and saving grace.

This saving and healing grace must always come to man as it truly is—as a gift of God's love. The sense of sin and need rules out the possibility of what Paul calls "boasting." (Rom 3,27) It makes it impossible for man to boast or be proud of any works of his by which he alone attains to salvation. Man must first acknowledge his weakness and sinfulness; in identifying this weakness, the Law "multiplied sin." It is only to the man who confesses his weakness that grace can come as the unmerited, free gift of a loving Father: "They are justified freely by his grace through the redemption which is in Christ Jesus. (Rom 3,24)

The Law then not only makes man aware of his own weakness. It forcefully teaches the truth which Paul sees as primary in the whole reality of grace and salvation: that these come to man wholly by God's gratuitous love. Man is saved by this creative love alone, not by the knowledge of, or obedience to, the Law. The recognition and acceptance in faith of the wholly gracious, completely transcendent, divine love revealed in Christ is central to Christianity. *Freedom from the Law means above all the humble and grateful recognition of the grace and power of God manifested not in the Law but in the person and works of Christ.* In the totality of the divine plan the regime of the Law was to be transitory, was to be fulfilled in Christ. The spiritual lesson of the gratuity and transcendence of grace is a lesson we may learn today by studying Paul's doctrine on the regime of Christ as a liberation from the Law. An understanding of the Law leads to grateful recognition and acceptance of the grace of Christ: "But before the faith [in Christ] came we were kept imprisoned under the Law, shut up for the faith that was to be revealed. Therefore the Law has been our tutor unto Christ, that we might be justified by faith." (Gal 3,23f)

Liberation from Death

Finally, St. Paul considers that Christ has freed man from that consequence of sin which is death. Death is always seen by Paul as the result of sin. As Christ conquers the principle of sin, he also brings victory over death. Today we seem to look at death in a more neutral sense, as the natural and inevitable consequence of man's composite structure of an immortal soul and a perishable body. We simply say that he is subject to death and destruction. The actual death, however, that man faces in this world is the result of sin. "As through one man sin entered into the world and through sin death, thus death has passed into all men because all have sinned." (Rom 5,12) Death as it actually is is man's enemy: a dark force which opposes him, intrudes ineluctably on his being, and faces him as darkness and a force destructive of life. Death is not a mere biological phenomenon to which man like all living things is subject; man's death is qualitatively different from that of plants and animals, and not only because he is a personal, incarnate spirit who endures bodily death. Death for man is "sinful," that is, it comes as the product of sin, as a reality which overtakes man as a thief in the night, violent and dark and bringing pain and dissolution. *29*

Death is the *de facto* concrete result of sin: first that of Adam, then that of each of us, who by his personal deeds of evil has participated in the sin of Adam and extended the dominion of sin. Without Christ death is darkness and the manifestation of eternal death, for man is created by God having as his only true and perfect good the destiny of grace and life in Christ. Death is an enemy of life in Christ because it is the conclusion of sin. It is the expression of man's condition without, and opposed to, grace or life in Christ, and comes as a penalty for sin: for the sin of Adam and for our own sins. "For the wages of sin is death." (Rom 6,23; cf. also Rom 6,16.21; 7,5.9f; 8,2.13; 1,32.) This does not mean that death is a merely arbitrary punishment of God, imposed like a fine or jail sentence by an angry Lord, but it does mean more than a mere biological necessity. Death is intrinsically related to sin. It is the expression of what sin is; sin is manifested fully in death.

Thus there is an essential, real difference between the death of the sinner and what St. Paul calls "death in the Lord." "But if we have died with Christ, we believe that we shall also live together with Christ." (Rom 6,8; cf. also 2 Tim 2,11; 1 Thes 4,16; 1 Cor 15,18.) The result of sin is death; a sinner's death is not like a dying in Christ. Death in Christ is a victory over that death which is a death *in* sin and *because of* sin. "Death is swallowed up in victory! O death where is thy victory? O death where is thy sting?" (1 Cor 15,55)

The death of the Christian is an act of consummation of the life of grace here on earth. It is a final giving over of self to Christ. It is the act in which a life in Christ culminates. Death in Christ is blessed and glorious. "Blessed are the dead who die in the Lord." (Ap 14,13) It is a share in the victory over death wrought in the death of Christ, in which the Christian participates. The whole outlook of Romans 6 makes us realize that our death is the completion of that incorporation into Christ's victorious death which has taken place at baptism. Paul sees the Christian as freed from death, for the sting of death is removed. Death becomes now a manifestation of grace and union in Christ. While physical death remains, it no longer has moral and real significance as the culminating act of sin. It is transformed into the culminating act on this earth of life in Christ victorious over sin and death. The divine power of the Father is manifested in the victory accomplished by Christ in his death, and this victory is the resurrection. So too, in and through Christ, by the Spirit, grace and the life of Christ are manifested in the death of the Christian which is a victory unto life everlasting. At the very moment when sin seems to conquer, sin and death are themselves conquered by the victorious grace of Christ.

The Christian is plunged into Christ's death; he is buried with Christ through baptism which is a real symbol of Christ's death. (Rom 6,3.4; Phil 3,10) In grace he rises to a new life in Christ. Through Christ's grace, death which is the consequence of sin becomes the supreme act of love and triumph in the power of the resurrection. The liberation from "the flesh" of death is here seen in its final effect. The life which is grace transforms the moment of sin in death, so that in death life can emerge victorious.

Paul's Summary

St. Paul has summarized the plight of man without Christ and without grace in a single sentence: "For when we were in the flesh the sinful passions, which were aroused by the Law, were at work in our members so that they brought forth fruit unto death." (Rom 7,5) Man without Christ is doomed to death because he is subject to and unable to control the sinful movements of the flesh, a principle of rebellion against God. In causing man to become more conscious of sin, the Law heightened his responsibility; but it gave no power to fulfill its own prescriptions. Even those Jews who, like the pharisees, took pride in their own ability to live out the Law are defeated by the Law, for grace comes only through Christ. Only through grace is man liberated from that bondage to Satan which leads to death. In his gracious mercy the Father has sent his Son to free man, to unite man with the living Trinity, to lead man to the plenitude of his destiny in the grace of Christ. (Ephesians 2 may be studied as a summary of this whole doctrine in Paul's own words and expression.)

LIFE IN CHRIST   The freeing of the Christian from the flesh, the Law, from sin and death, is always an introduction into a realm of the Spirit, a kingdom of grace and life. Indeed it is a re-creation of man by the healing and saving power of grace, won for us in the death and resurrection of Christ. We shall turn our attention now to the description by St. Paul of the positive aspects of the work of Christ, which is the actual communication to us of the life of grace. This will be an attempt to outline the richness of meaning which St. Paul expresses in these words: "If then any man is in Christ, he is a new creature." (2 Cor 5,17) Because the Christian is in Christ he is a new being: not new in his natural being as such, but new in the life of God and in the supernatural order. Because he is possessed of a new life, he is in Christ, and thus in a new relationship with God. The positive aspect, then, of the work of grace will involve an inner transformation which amounts to a new creation. It will mean a new presence of God to man and of man to the loving God who saves him.

JUSTIFICATION   St. Paul often uses the words "just" and "justice" of genuine religion and its true followers. This use is in accord with the usual and general scriptural meaning of these terms. Justification, especially in Paul's epistles to the Romans and to the Galatians, is the process or the action by which God sanctifies man, that is, by which God makes man pleasing to him. The notion may be extended to the use of the term justice as a designation of the whole inner reality of the Christian life of grace. St. Paul recalls the sanctification or justification of Abraham, who appears as the symbol or the great example in the Old Testament of the bestowal of gratuitous grace by God: "Even thus, 'Abraham believed God, and it was credited to him as justice.' [Gen 15,6] Know therefore that the men of faith are the real sons of Abraham." (Gal 3,6f) An understanding of Abraham's faith and his justification before God is thus set forth by Paul as a way of seeing the sanctification of the Christian, who must be justified by God as was Abraham: "For there is no distinction, as all have sinned and have need of the glory of God. They are justified freely by his grace through the redemption which is in Christ Jesus. . . ." (Rom 3,22–24)

Paul is writing to oppose those Jews and Christians who saw justification as something to be accomplished by a person through his own good works. In this aberration, man was seen as bringing about grace as a reward or even as a salary from God for good deeds done. Paul vigorously opposes this religion of human self-sufficiency, denying, as we have seen, man's power to perform the good works of the Law, and constantly affirming that justification is a work of God bestowed on faithful men as a free divine gift. The Apostle strongly opposes a religion based on "boasting," on self-sufficiency before God. Such a religion is injurious to the divine goodness and is based on an unreal view of the human condition.

It is in this context that the example of Abraham is proposed. "What then shall we say that Abraham . . . acquired? For if Abraham was justified by works, he has reason to boast, but not before God. For what does Scripture say? 'Abraham believed God and it was credited to him as justice.' Now to him who works, the reward is not credited as a favor but as something due. But to him who does not work, but believes in him who justified the impious, his faith is credited to him as justice." (Rom 4,1–5) Abraham was truly a just man before God. How had this come

32

about? St. Paul describes two ways of receiving something: in the first, recompense is given for work accomplished; in the other a pure gift is bestowed. The justice of Abraham was a gift that was bestowed as really as a payment rendered for services, but was nevertheless in no way dependent on Abraham's merits or his work. Not even faith was a good work meriting grace: "For by grace you have been saved through faith; and that not from yourselves, for it is the gift of God; not as the outcome of works, lest anyone may boast." (Eph 2,8f) Faith in St. Paul is indeed hearing the divine message and accepting it (Rom 1,17; 10,14–21; 1 Thes 1,3–10; 1 Cor 2,5; Eph 1,13); it is an obedience to the divine authority. (Rom 1,5; 16,26; 2 Cor 10,5f) It is, moreover, the commitment and surrender of all that a man is to God, this commitment and openness to God is *itself* the work of grace. Faith, then, becomes the act of grace by which man is enabled to cooperate with the justifying power of God.

THE ROLE OF FAITH   This role of faith is stressed in Romans 4, 17–25, a passage based upon God's promise to Abraham of a son and numerous progeny. The latter seemed impossible, for Abraham was old and Sara his wife was sterile. Abraham believed, however, "hoping against hope," and did not "waver through unbelief but was strengthened in faith, giving glory to God." God's promises were sufficient foundation for Abraham's faith, and reliance, and perfect commitment. Abraham's faith was in no sense a "good work" he performed on his own strength; it was an act of reliance and confidence in God's power and goodness. In this act of cooperation with grace, Abraham is justified before God. He receives grace, but receives it freely as a gift. The living faith by which Abraham entrusts himself to God is the conscious, free response of cooperation with the transforming power of God. This is the interpretation of St. Thomas Aquinas: "It is not that by faith we have merited our justification in some way. Rather it is that in this same justification, by which we are justified by God, the first movement of our spirit to God is by faith. Thus faith itself, as being the first part of justice, comes to us from God and a living faith." God makes man pleasing to himself only in and through man's free cooperation in faith, by which man opens himself to the gift of God and accepts it wholeheartedly.

What is the reality of the justification accorded by God when man cooperates in faith? Is it merely like a statement of God declaring the sinner just? Or is it a divine act by which the sinner is internally transformed and becomes a new reality before God? Catholic thought has always been that the justice bestowed on man is a gratuitous gift (Gal 3,6ff), and a true justice which actually transforms man into a person pleasing to God. St. Paul links justice and justification with sanctification and purification (1 Cor 6,11), and sees the justified man as living a new life in Christ. (Rom 6,15–23; 3,21–26) The liberation from sin and death, already described, is a spiritual reality which is accomplished in man by grace at the moment of justification. Its effect is to introduce man into a genuine state of justice. This new life is indeed life in Christ, so real that Paul can say: "With Christ I am nailed to the cross. It is now no longer I that live, but Christ lives in me. And the life that I now live in the flesh, I live in the faith of the Son of God." (Gal 2,19f)

Thus justification initiates a new life which is a sharing by the Christian in the life of Christ himself. St. Paul teaches as clearly as does St. John that grace is a new existence communicated in the power of the death and resurrection of Christ. The whole of Romans 6 may be read at this point. It summarizes Paul's realistic understanding of the incorporation into Christ, the dying to sin and rising to a new life, which is accomplished in the process of justification.

NEWNESS OF LIFE   Justification is thus synonymous with the communication of new life in Christ to the Christian. St. Paul frequently contrasts the "old man" of sin and the flesh with the "new man" who is spiritual and dedicated to a fundamental holiness. "If any man is in Christ, he is a new creature." (2 Cor 5,17; cf. Gal 6,15.) Because God has created us "in Christ Jesus" (Eph 2,10), the Christian is to live this new life. "But be renewed in the spirit of your mind, and put on the new man, which has been created according to God in justice and holiness of truth." (Eph 4,23f; cf. Col 3,10.) The liturgy of Easter is especially devoted to this theme of new life won for us in Christ, and communicated to us in the sacraments. Entrance into the Christian life is truly a "regeneration" and a "renewal": the equivalent of being "justified by his grace." (Ti 3,6f) Just as in the third chapter of John's gospel we saw how real was the notion of rebirth, so Paul stresses this point, that the Christians to whom he writes may be thoroughly convinced of the mysterious and hidden, yet actual, presence of grace. This conviction in them will lead, in turn, to their living in the light (Eph 5,8f), to action which gives expression to the new "reality" which Christians have become.

34   St. Paul is surely not speaking of grace as something unreal and fanciful. True, what he says is incomprehensible to the "old man" who

is incapable of an understanding enlightened by faith. But to the eyes of faith Paul presents in the most forceful manner possible the genuine reality of the transformation that grace effects. This is never presented merely as an abstraction, or as something reserved to a special few who have some emotional or sentimental religious feelings. Paul presents the reality of grace to every Christian in terms of a demand for gratitude to God, expressed in everyday moral behavior. He is well aware, as all his letters attest, that this new life is lived in the world. (1 Cor 5,10) But the Christian can live this life of Christ in his daily situation by becoming conscious of what he is. He can give expression to his baptism by a life which is not under the domination of evil, not subject to any standards but those compatible with his allegiance to Christ. The existence of weakness and evil among Christians is no excuse for St. Paul to cease preaching his divine message with its moral demands.

SONS OF GOD BY ADOPTION   The reality of the new being of the Christian is also portrayed by St. Paul as an extension or participation in Christ's personal being as Son of the Father. The Christian, united to Christ, is truly a son of God in virtue of possessing the divine reality of grace. That he is a son of God is the result of a rebirth by which the divine life is communicated to him. "But when the fullness of time came, God sent his Son . . . that he might redeem those who were under the Law, that we might receive the adoption of sons. And because you are sons, God has sent the Spirit of his Son into our hearts crying 'Abba, Father,' so that he is no longer a slave, but a son; and if a son, an heir also through God." (Gal 4,5–7; cf. Rom 8, 14–17.)

Just as the synoptic gospels presented our Lord inculcating the notion of God as Father, so does St. Paul insist on the fact that by grace we have entered into new relations with God in virtue of an adopted sonship in Christ. By grace we are joined to Christ and thus related as sons, as children to the Father in heaven. Since this is the fact of the Christian condition, the Christian can behave toward God as a child would to a Father who is loving, merciful, and powerful. Initiation into Christ is a being taken into the life of the Trinity. The Christian has relations with God which go beyond those of creature to Creator. They are those of son to Father, of two persons who enter into mutual communion which is a genuine friendship. We no longer approach God only as the Lord of the world, as the distant and omnipotent Creator; we deal with him as someone pre-eminently personal who has by grace willed to take us into his own divine life. The destiny of man is realized   35
only in this order of personal relationship with God, initiated in the life

of grace. "God is trustworthy, by him you have been called into fellowship with his Son, Jesus Christ our Lord." (1 Cor 1,9)

IN CHRIST   If we are related as sons to the Father, it is because of a union with Christ so intimate that it appears to St. Paul as an identification of Christ with each Christian. (Cf. Ac 22,7f.) Thus the Apostle realizes that Christ lives in him and that the Christian is "in Christ." "For you are all the children of God through faith in Christ Jesus. For all you who have been baptized into Christ have put on Christ." (Gal 3,26f) Sharing in the reality of Christ is the innermost principle of the Christian life; it is, in the terms of later theology, a sharing in the being of God himself, in the reality of Christ through the power of the Spirit. All Christian life is but an expression of this fundamental reality, so that the basic morality of the Christian is found not in the Law but in being true to what one is through the grace of Christ. To be "in Christ" according to Paul is not merely to profess faith in him, to adhere to his teachings, or even to be attached to Christ by personal admiration. It is much more profound. *It is to be one with him.*

"Thus do you consider yourselves also as dead to sin, but alive to God in Christ Jesus." (Rom 6,11; cf. 1 Cor 1,30.) A new existence has been received by the Christian, so that he lives in Christ. This does not mean, of course, some sort of mystical or real absorption into Christ so that the human self disappears. It does mean a real sharing in the life which is proper to Christ alone, the Son of the living Father. It means a new creation in man by the reception of grace, and a new, conscious mode of existence in which Christ becomes in a real sense the center and focus of the Christian's life. It means too that the Christian, in Christ, is aware of and gives full acceptance to Christ's own devotion and openness to the Father. "May Christ dwell through faith in your hearts." (Eph 3,17) Christians share by grace in the sonship of Christ, and by faith and love are enabled to participate in the sentiments of the Lord. (Cf. Rom 15,5–7.)

All this is the work of the Spirit. (1 Cor 6,11; Eph 4,30) "The charity of God is poured forth in our hearts by the Holy Spirit who has been given to us." (Rom 5,5) The Spirit who lives in the Christian makes him a son with the Son. He is made in the image of the Son according to the eternal will of the Father. (Rom 8,29) This new life is consciously realized in faith and love, though it is rooted in the transforming adoption of the Christian into Christ in what theology calls "the bestowing of sanctifying grace." The conscious dimension of this new life is spoken of by St. Paul: "For none of us lives to himself,

36

and none dies to himself; for if we live, we live to the Lord, or if we die, we die to the Lord. Therefore, whether we live or die, we are the Lord's." (Rom 14,7f)

The Christian has "put on" Christ (Rom 13,12–14) and lives conscious of his relation to the Father. As St. Thomas has said, our total love for God is expressed, at least habitually, by loving nothing or no one more than God. (S. Th., 2ª2ᵃᵉ, 44,4, ad 2) This does not mean a love or an awareness which is always explicitly conscious of God; such is not necessary or even possible in this life. What is meant by St. Paul, and then by St. Thomas, is that the Christian in virtue of what he has become through grace will not renounce God, nor prefer anything of this world to God. The root of this new life and awareness is the transformation described in Romans 6. (Cf. Gal 4,19; Col 1,27; Rom 8,9–11.)

Life in Christ is thus realized in the radical transformation of the Christian from a son of wrath and sin into a son of the Father, a brother of Christ. This new being is consciously expressed by sharing not only in the knowledge of Christ, but in his sentiments, and in his conscious love for the Father. The Christian is constantly alert to this reality. His life becomes progressively more deeply rooted in grace, in his being in Christ.

IN THE BODY OF CHRIST   Receiving the life of God and being incorporated into Christ are personal acts; we accept Christ by faith, and go out to him in charity. Yet we receive and are united to Christ not in isolation, but as social beings. There is a sharing of Christ's life in the Church which is his body. We do not intend here to develop the Pauline teaching on the mystical body of Christ, but only to point out the Christian fact that grace is not the grace of Christ only, but the grace of Christ in his Church. All grace, as it is the grace *of* Christ and *in* Christ, is grace in the Church. There are not two ways of grace: personal and ecclesial, individual and social, but one. We live in Christ in the Church and are united in the Church to Christ.

The Church which is God's people, summoned and called by him in Christ, is the source of grace. It is the setting for the life of grace. St. Paul stresses both the union of all peoples in the Church (Rom 11,5.17–24; Gal 6,15) and the fact that in Christ all men are called to salvation through grace. But Christ unites men to himself by uniting them to his Church—the society of those who truly believe in him. All of us, in our diversity and our differences, are united in the one body of Christ. 37 (Rom 12,4–8; cf. 1 Cor 12,12–31.) The Spirit is the principle of this unity of all in Christ, just as he is the principle of our incorporation into Christ. "For in one Spirit we were all baptized into one body . . . and we were all given to drink of one Spirit." (1 Cor 12,13; cf. Eph. 2,22; 4,4.) And this body is Christ. "For as the body is one and has many members, and all the members of the body, many as they are, form one body, so also is it with Christ." (1 Cor 12,12) The Church is the body of Christ (Eph 1,23) and the Christian's incorporation into Christ is at once an incorporation into the Church.

Conclusion

Our life of grace then is a life in Christ in the Church. We live to Christ by a life in the society of the faithful people of God which is Christ's body. This of course does not mean that the individual and the personal is to be obscured by the social. It does mean, however, that all our life as Christians is a life lived as members of the society which is Christ's body. Christ without the Church is "incomplete." Paul sees Christ as a "collective person" which is the fullness of the Church united as members of the body of which he is the head. The principle of union of all in Christ is the common sharing of the life of Christ (at least by faith.) The Church is not the body of the Father but of Christ, in whom all things are created (Col 1,16); as head of the body Christ is distinct from it, though he is also united with it. The body is united in the Spirit, its soul and source of union and unity. The Church is the continuance of the incarnation; it is the body of all who love Christ and live in him. We may recognize in the life of grace a divine force which unites us to the body of Christ existing here and now in the world as the Church. The Church is the *locus,* the setting, the mystical body, in which the Father vivifies us by uniting us to the life of his Son, in the vital efficacy of the Spirit. Our salvation, our life in the world, our final destiny is worked out by union with Christ, living in his body, his Church.

But God, who is rich in mercy, by reason of his very great love wherewith he has loved us even when we were dead by reason of our sins, brought us to life together with Christ (by grace you have been saved), and raised us up together, and seated us together in heaven in Christ Jesus, that he might show in the ages to come the overflowing riches of his grace in kindness towards us in Christ Jesus. For by grace you have been saved through faith; and that not from yourselves, for it is the gift of God; not as the outcome of works, lest anyone should boast. For his workmanship we are, created in

Christ Jesus in good works, which God has made ready beforehand that we may walk in them. . . . And coming, he announced the good tidings of peace to you who were afar off, and of peace to those who were near; because through him we both have access in one Spirit to the Father. Therefore, you are now no longer strangers and foreigners, but you are citizens with the saints and members of God's household: you are built upon the foundation of the apostles and prophets with Christ Jesus himself as the chief corner stone. In him the whole structure is closely fitted together and grows into a temple holy in the Lord; in him you too are being built together into a dwelling place for God in the Spirit. (Eph 2,4–10.17–22)

"One body and one Spirit, even as you were called in one hope of your calling: one Lord, one faith, one baptism; one God and Father of all, who is above all, and throughout all, and in us all." (Eph 4,4–6)

Note: Chapters 5 through 8 of the epistle to the Romans is a longer summary of Paul's doctrine of grace, justification, new life in Christ: in these chapters may be seen all the elements of the foregoing exposition. A detailed reading and study of these chapters will provide a useful review of New Testament teaching on grace.

Note on 2 Peter 1,3f   For indeed his divine power has granted us all things pertaining to life and piety through the knowledge of him who has called us by his own glory and power—through which he has granted us the very great and precious promises, so that through them you may become partakers of the divine nature, having escaped from the corruption of that lust which is in the world.

This is one of the most famous New Testament passages on the life of grace. It asserts the initiative of the loving God, his plan for human salvation, and the necessity of faith to receive the benefits of the divine promises. The text then tells us that through God's glory and power, in virtue of the divine promises, man is to become a partaker of the divine nature. This is not meant in a merely external sense, that is, man imitating God from the outside, as it were; nor is it a quasi-pantheistic statement pointing to some sort of absorption of man into the divinity. It is a reassertion in clear terms of what has already been seen of man's incorporation into the life and light which is God. It is a statement of the Christian's union with Christ and of his reception, through the Spirit, of a new and divine principle of life. Because this text expresses so vividly the reality of grace, it has become a classic theological text for substantiating the doctrine of sanctifying grace defined as a 39 sharing in the life and proper reality of God himself.

CHAPTER TWO

CHURCH
TEACHING
ON GRACE

Through the liturgy and in her preaching and teaching the Church has continued to present the revealed doctrine of grace as found in the New Testament writers. In the administration of the sacraments, and through the varied activities in her daily life, the Church has kept alive the life of grace; she has given to men the necessary means for acquiring, regaining, and increasing union with Christ. The life of the

Church is thus a constant "activating" of the work of the redemption carried on in human history for all men. For our purposes, the activity of the Church may be considered twofold—that of preaching the Word of God, and of communicating the life of grace through the sacred liturgy and all the forms of Christian living which express the historic reality of the incarnation. For the present we shall examine the teaching of the Church as it concerns safeguarding the purity of faith in respect to the doctrines of salvation and grace. This will consist of a brief look at some of the major doctrinal decisions made by the Church in opposition to critical heresies which sprang up during the course of the Church's existence.

It must not be forgotten, of course, that in these controversies the Church is concerned with a strong affirmative statement of certain truths denied or misinterpreted by heretical teaching. These solemn affirmations of Catholic dogma do not intend to embrace all Catholic teaching on the subject. The definitions of certain crucial doctrines are solemn reaffirmations of what has been received by the Church in the total revelation of the apostolic age. The whole of the New Testament teaching on grace is the foundation of all subsequent Catholic teaching. The Church of today presents us with this teaching, as well as with the definitions she has advanced to clarify and safeguard New Testament teaching itself. A survey of some major heretical movements will enable us to see which points of scriptural doctrine have been emphasized through the course of the Church's history.

It is well to recall the importance of a study of orthodox religious doctrine. The acceptance of orthodoxy is a matter of obedience in faith to the divine truth presented in the preaching of Christ and his Church. Through the submission of our minds to God's truth, we acquire a knowledge of divine reality in the form of doctrinal statements expressed in human words. But faith is not only an acceptance of words; it is also an assent of the whole person to the realities conveyed in these words. What we do in fact is attain to the realities of revelation in and through the knowledge of truth contained in the statements of the teaching Church. This means that only in the purity of Catholic (that is, complete, total) faith are we assured religious contact with the realities of God. Our Catholic assent to the Church's teaching on grace is not merely a matter of obedience to her teaching authority and that of Christ. It is more. It is our assurance that through the acceptance of divine truth we will also have access to divine reality. Our religious grasp of the reality of grace is thus contingent upon our intellectual assent to divine truth. The whole theology of faith indicates that our assent to divine truth is an actual contact with divine reality; only in orthodox truth, moreover, are we assured of a genuine contact with these realities of revelation and redemption.

ST. AUGUSTINE, THE DOCTOR OF GRACE

The theological work of St. Augustine of Hippo covers the entire range of Christian belief. His profound thought has resulted in a great many positions and points of view which have become decisive for all later Western thought. Because of his particular concern for the doctrine of salvation, and owing to his many polemical works against the Pelagian heresy, he is in a special way the "Doctor of Grace." Augustine's defense of the true Catholic doctrine on the divine initiative in the work of salvation, on the inability of man to achieve his own eternal glory, and on the doctrines of original sin, freedom, and predestination, has become a cornerstone for all Catholic thought.

The immediate concern of this chapter will be to outline some typical Augustinian positions on selected questions of grace. The theology of original sin and divine predestination are treated in other volumes in this series.

Whereas Augustine is known especially for his defense of Catholic doctrine against Pelagianism, his doctrine on grace is not wholly contained in the range of this controversy on free will and the necessity of grace for salvation. The broader aspects of the whole theology of grace are present in Augustine's writings throughout. Thus the great doctor constantly emphasizes the fundamental doctrine of our incorporation into Christ, and the fact that by grace we become sons of God and are admitted into a sharing of the divine nature. All of this is developed in a typical Augustinian doctrine, that of God's presence in the depths of the soul, or in his treatment of the presence of the soul to God, a constant echo of Johannine and Pauline themes.

Man United to Christ

This typical and characteristic doctrine of interiority and presence is a favorite and even dominant theme of Augustine. It expresses admirably his own profound point of view on the nearness and "availability" of God to the Christian soul. This thought is carried further in Augustine's development of the doctrine of the mystical body or the total Christ: "Not Christ in the head and not in the body, but the total

42

Christ in head and body." (*On John*, XXVIII, 1; *PL*35, 1622) The Christian is so united to Christ as to be one with him in his body the Church. Augustine sees the whole work of redemption as a saving union effected by Christ with the Christian, in virtue of which the Christian enters into relations of particular interior intimacy with God. Man's deepest longings and profoundest needs are fulfilled by the loving graciousness of God, who has united man to himself in Christ through the Church. Such supernatural fulfillment is possible to man only through Christ. The whole of Augustine's *Confessions* is a rendering of thanks to God for leading him through devious paths to Christ. In his passionate search for God, in the depths of his realization of his own weakness, Augustine experienced at once man's hopelessness without God and his need of God's grace if he is to achieve his true destiny of perfect happiness. Augustine's own bitter experience of his misery without God made him fully aware of the liberating, healing, saving, and redemptive aspects of divine grace. His development of this doctrine is his special glory and personal contribution to our religious heritage.

Fallen Man

Augustine was especially conscious of man's existence in a fallen state—the just punishment for Adam's rebellion against God: "Because it was through free choice that he abandoned God, he underwent the just judgment of God." (*On Correption and Grace*, X, 28; *PL*44, 933) After the fall, man is no longer capable of pleasing God without the new and creative power of grace. His nature and powers have been greatly weakened and turned from God to the pursuit of evil. The grace which God bestows in Christ is totally gratuitous, the result of divine love alone. It is impossible for man to attain it without the merciful intervention of God. Only by God's free gift is the salvation of fallen man possible. This grace Augustine sees as the divine correction, wholly gratuitous, of the evil results of man's sins. The restoration to man of supernatural grace, lost by the sin of Adam, amounts to a new creation in the power of Christ's merits and redemption. Without grace, man remains subject to the flesh, to sin, and to the death which sin brings.

Like St. Paul, St. Augustine stresses the bondage of man without Christ and his need of liberation in the grace of Christ. Indeed, the liberty to do what is good in the order of salvation is itself the fruit of a liberation from the power of sin. This liberation is entirely the work of God's grace. It cannot be produced or merited by man; it comes to him as the result of a loving divine initiative. Liberty for Augustine is some- *43* thing more than the mere possession of free will or choice. It is the power to do the good we will. (Cf. Rom 7,13–25.) Sinful man does not have this power of his own. He is incapable of the goods of salvation. Although all his acts are not evil, no single one is capable of being supernaturally or perfectly good. The observance of the moral good necessary to salvation is impossible to fallen man, who lacks liberty in the sense just defined. He must receive this true liberty from healing and saving grace. It is on this point that the Pelagian controversy centers.

PELAGIANISM

The chief heresy on grace takes its name from the British monk Pelagius, a holy and rigorously ascetical man who preached his doctrines from about 405 A.D. in Rome, Africa, and in the East, Palestine. His teachings were taken up by Coelestius, and especially by Julian, Bishop of Eclana. The heretical positions advanced were condemned by councils in Carthage and Milevis, and by Popes Innocent I and Zosimus. The key point of the Pelagian doctrine—worked out in greater detail by Julian of Eclana than by Pelagius himself—is that of the self-sufficiency of man's unhampered liberty. By his liberty man is set free from God; after bestowing liberty on man in creation, God can only influence man's action as a judge approving or condemning what an emancipated human freedom has chosen.

Free Will

Man's free will is totally unaffected by sin, which is seen as merely a wrong choice with no lasting or harmful consequences. Thus, in effect, this system denies the reality and effects of original sin; in consequence, it denies the need for a saving, redeeming grace. Grace is hardly needed for man or human nature, since sin has left nature unaffected and in full possession of a self-sufficient liberty. Nature is capable of attaining salvation through its own efforts. Man in consequence does not need an inner, redeeming grace. Grace for Pelagius was merely a juridical forgiveness of sins, a gracious pardon, not an interior transformation of man who stands in real need of such divine help. The passion and death of Christ are not considered necessary for the redemption of man from within by the bestowal of healing grace; these deeds of Christ are only manifestations of God's love for man, offering him a good moral example. The death of Christ need not be anything more than this, for in

44

the Pelagian hypothesis man really is in no need of inner transformation or renovation by grace. He possesses fully a powerful liberty capable on its own of all necessary good acts.

Naturalism

We may call Pelagianism a "naturalism," for according to it intrinsically supernatural grace is not necessary for man's salvation. This heresy sees man as endowed with a liberty capable of fulfilling the whole moral law by its own resources. This liberty can obtain salvation as the just reward for right choices made by man alone, wholly without God's inner grace. The Pelagians called "graces" such external helps to goodness as the life and example of Christ, the teaching of Scripture, and other like aids which do not affect man from within. The system resembles that of the pharisees who felt entirely capable of observing the whole Law and who boasted of their own good works. (In this sense we have seen Paul rule out "boasting".) Pelagianism rests on a false notion of liberty, which is seen as a power making man independent of God. It is a power over which God's grace has no influence, being wholly unaffected by sin whether original or personal. Thus there is a radical denial of the necessity of grace and genuine redemption.

Pelagianism overlooks the profound struggle within man between good and evil. (Rom 7,19–25) It is far from the words of Paul: "Or what have you that you have not received?" (1 Cor 4,7), or of St. John: "For without me you can do nothing." (Jn 15,5)

Saving Grace

For the Pelagians, who denied the reality of the need for grace in the Catholic sense, free will itself was the primary "grace"; it sufficed by itself, it "emancipated" from God. All else in the order of salvation was merit or due recompense, a salary owed to a faithful and good servant; thus it was not grace, not free, unmerited, and gratuitous. The entirety of Augustine's theological understanding of the faith, and indeed the whole of his own personal experience in the ways of sin and grace, opposed the Pelagian system. If, in Augustine's vigorous reaction to Pelagianism, there are imperfections and failures to make clear distinctions, his response is fundamentally that of the true faith. Man is capable only of that good which God makes him capable of: "Give me what you ask, and ask what you will." (*Confessions*, VII,21,27) All centers on this for Augustine. Man cannot move toward God; he is incapable of taking a step to accomplish his own salvation without the gracious, free help of God: "Grace is given us by Jesus Christ, our Lord, that by it the law may be accomplished, nature freed, and sin conquered." (*On Grace and Free Will*, XIV,27: PL44,897)

Grace does not do away with free will; this to St. Augustine would be a ridiculous view, for then grace would destroy what it was meant to perfect. Grace heals and gives power to the faculty of choice. It gives a liberty which is also the capability to do good by following Christ. This grace is bestowed not for any merits or good works of man, for sinful man does not merit his own supernatural destiny, but out of the largesse of divine love alone..With grace man can merit, without grace he cannot. God's grace is given to enable man to act well, not to take away his free will. Without this grace, man remains a "son of wrath," an enemy of God, still subject to sin and spiritual death. Man can sin on his own power, but he cannot recover from sin unless the loving hand of God assists him internally. Augustine firmly and triumphantly asserts the transcendence of God, his love and mercy, the reality of redemption and of grace. Thus in defending the only true religious relation of sinful man to his God and Redeemer, he defends orthodox doctrine.

Early Councils

In a number of fifth-century councils the Church consecrated various Augustinian formulas and statements, using them to express her own divine faith. The dependence of man on the transcendent divine causality, made real in the order of grace, is one of the things affirmed: "God works in man many good things which do not depend on man [which man himself does not produce], but man does nothing good which God does not give him the power to do." (D193; II Council of Orange, Can. 20, A.D. 529: taken from St. Augustine, *Against Two Letters of Pelagius*, IX, 21; PL44,586.) In this passage is affirmed the need on man's part of grace and divine assistance for all good works. Augustine did not clearly distinguish what we would call God's natural assistance, by which all beings in creation are maintained in existence and action, from his supernatural grace, by which men are enabled to do good works beyond the power and capability of nature. Yet in the context of the Pelagian controversy this text applies primarily to the need of genuine supernatural grace for good moral action. The council thus uses Augustine's words to affirm a fundamental element of Catholic teaching on the real need of grace.

46

The Council of Carthage condemns those (the Pelagians) who

hold that grace "has the power only for the forgiveness of sins . . . and is not also an assistance to avoid sins in the future." (D103, Can. 3) This denies the Pelagian position that grace is only a forgiveness of sin granted after a wrong use of freedom; it likewise denies the Pelagian understanding of forgiveness as something merely external or juridical. The council goes on to affirm that grace is a gift and an aid in the effort to avoid sin. In its fourth canon the council condemns the purely external Pelagian understanding of grace. Convicted of error are those who would say "that God's grace through Jesus Christ our Lord helps us avoid sin solely because it gives us a clear knowledge . . . of . . . the commandments, but deny that through this grace there is given to us an *ability* and a love of doing what we know should be done." (D104; *TCT*528)

The view of the Pelagians that grace is merely something which makes easier the doing of what is good, "as if to say that if grace were not given, it would be, not indeed easy, but truly possible to obey God's commandments without grace" (D105; *TCT*529, Can. 5) is likewise declared to be false and heretical. Thus grace is not something merely pleasant and helpful. *It is in fact demanded if man is to observe the commandments and lead a good life.*

The "Catalogue of Errors," called in Latin *Indiculus de Gratia Dei,* was a collection of statements drawn up perhaps by St. Prosper of Aquitaine and then universally accepted as giving true Catholic teaching. The following brief extracts oppose the Pelagian doctrine:

"No one is capable of rising from the depths of this loss [in original sin] by his own free will, if the grace of the merciful God does not lift him up." (D130; *TCT*368) "Unless He alone who is good [God himself] grants a *participation of himself,* no one of himself is good." (D131; cf. *TCT*534.) This document then affirms the need of the daily help of grace for the living of the good life (D132; *TCT*535), and goes on to say: "All the efforts, and all the works and merits of the saints must be attributed to . . . God, because no one can please God with anything that is not his own gift." (D134; *TCT*536) The whole matter is thus summarized: "God so works in the hearts of man and in free will that the holy thought, the religious purpose, and every movement of a good will are from God, because it is through him that we can do any good, and without him we can do nothing." (D135; cf. *TCT*537.)

The solemn voice of the Church here approves the intuitions of St. Augustine in condemning Pelagianism as a system which destroys the heart of the reality of divine grace. The Catholic, therefore, professes his dependence on the love and mercy of God, in virtue of which alone he is redeemed and given the real, internal help of grace to live a life pleasing to God. In his whole religious attitude the Catholic acknowledges that he is saved not by his own power, not through his "independent" free will and strength, but through the grace of Christ.

Thus in the fifth century did the Church through her councils and bishops, and through the profound religious mind of Augustine, reassert the basic truths taught in the New Testament. It is only in acknowledging by faith the truth of our own reality in relation to God that we become fully ourselves, and alive in the grace of God.

SEMI-PELAGIANISM

In opposition to some of Augustine's thought, but owing also in part to misunderstandings of some of his polemical positions, there were those in the fifth century who felt that man's freedom had been excessively limited by Augustine and that his doctrine on predestination removed all possibility of an initial, free cooperation of man with grace. To defend their view of these questions, the so-called semi-Pelagians, centered in monastic circles of southern France, thought it necessary to reserve at least the first step toward grace to man: to see in the initial conversion of man to the life of grace a movement wholly dependent on man's free will and natural goodness. Put another way, the position of semi-Pelagians denied the need of grace for the initial conversion of man's free will and natural goodness. In other words, the semi-Pelagians denied the need of grace for the initial conversion of man to God. There was error in the failure to recognize that the whole process of man's salvation from the moment of first conversion to that of final perseverance is the result of God's grace. Salvation is an entirely gratuitous gift which enables man to take even the first step toward God; it enables him thereafter to act well and to persevere in grace. It is this total need for grace which the Church reaffirmed on the occasion of the semi-Pelagian heresy.

The Church's Teaching

The position of the Church is found in the "Catalogue of Errors" (*Indiculus*) previously mentioned. Again the fundamental insights of St. Augustine are used to express the Catholic teaching:

48

We profess that God is the author of all good desires and deeds, of all efforts and virtues, with which from the *beginning of faith* man tends to God. And we do not doubt that his grace *anticipates* every one of man's merits, and that it is through him that we *begin* both the will and the performance of any good work. To be sure, free will is not destroyed by this help and strength from God, but it is freed; so that from darkness it is brought to light, from evil to good, from sickness to health, from ignorance to prudence. For such is God's goodness to men that he wills that his gifts be our merits, and that he will grant us an eternal reward for what he has given us. Indeed, God so acts in us that we both will and do what he wills. . . . And he acts in this manner so that we are cooperators with his grace. (D141; *TCT*542)

The Second Council of Orange (in southern France, A.D. 529) made particularly clear the Church's condemnation of the semi-Pelagians. The decisions of the council were approved by Pope Boniface II in A.D. 531. The council teaches that "even the desire to be cleansed [from sin] is accomplished through the infusion and the interior working of the Holy Spirit." (D177; *TCT*544, Can. 4) Furthermore, the first beginnings of conversion to God are the work of his grace, so that the "grace of faith is not found in the free will of all who desire to be baptized, but is conferred through the generosity of Christ." (D199; *TCT*548; cf. D178f; *TCT*545f.) The true doctrine is summarized thus:

We also believe and profess for our salvation that in every good work it is not that we make a beginning and afterwards are helped through God's mercy, but rather, that without any previous good merits on our part, God himself first inspires us with faith in him and love of him so that we may faithfully seek the sacrament of baptism, and so that after baptism, with his help, we may be able to accomplish what is pleasing to him. (D200; *TCT*549)

Thus it is clearly Catholic teaching that God anticipates our good works by his grace, and that our union with him is the effect of his gifts to us. God does not destroy free will, but so gives his grace that we cooperate freely with it. In the thought of St. Augustine, we thus acquire true freedom: a delivery from the slavery of sin. Yet if man cooperates, and is never merely a dumb or passive tool of God's, he yet depends on God's grace for the entire work of salvation. The Church in the fifth century thus gave definitive expression to the reality of man's relationship of grateful dependence on the gratuitous love of God.

Summary

These statements of the Church are not merely affirmations of divine truth. They are also proclamations of divine mercy. In accepting these truths the Catholic bespeaks his gratitude to God and becomes properly disposed to live the life of grace. The religious intuition of Pelagianism and semi-Pelagianism was primarily a declaration of the need for emphasis upon man's role in salvation; but the intuition was exaggerated to exalt man's supposed independence and liberty at the expense of the divine sovereignty and transcendence. In opposition to the false emphasis of the Pelagians, the Church upholds man's genuine cooperation with grace, but exalts to its necessary and proper place the divine primacy and the reality of grace. Fundamentally Pelagianism, in seeking to appreciate man's activity and freedom, destroyed the basis of that free action by denying its roots in the grace of God. By thus denying the true source of human greatness and freedom, Pelagianism undermined its own position. The Church's affirmation of the primacy and necessity of internal grace is at once a vindication of the divine role in salvation and a guarantee of the reality of man's cooperation. The religious relationship of man to God is assured only on the basis of a profession of the true faith.

THE COUNCIL OF TRENT AND THE REFORMATION

The following exposition of the teaching of the Council of Trent is concerned with Catholic reaction to the heretical positions of Reformation theology. It is not intended to indicate that contemporary Protestants hold positions unchanged from those of the Reformers. Our one concern is with the understanding of the teaching of the Council of Trent in its own context—the age of the Reformation.

In speaking of the reaction of the Church to Protestantism our attention will be focused solely on certain central points of Catholic teaching which were enunciated at the Council of Trent, principally against the errors of Martin Luther. Lutheranism can be understood as resting upon several basic religious intuitions which serve as generating principles for doctrine on grace and all the rest of Luther's salvation. Our immediate concern is not with the historical development and forms of Protestantism, but with the traditional Catholic understanding of salvation, and its relation to the distinctively Lutheran understanding of grace. Luther may be seen not so much as a systematic theologian but as a man with extraordinary religious sensibility. In terms of his religious experience he proposed an interpretation of the Christian religion which in essential issues is at variance with the Catholic faith.

There is question here of more than verbal or abstract differences of opinion; the problem involves two different ways of realizing and living man's religious relation to God in Christ. It will be seen that Lutheran ideas are directly opposed to those of Pelagianism.

Man and God

Luther's concept of man's relationship with God is of utmost importance and is central to his whole thought. Seeking above all, it seems, certitude and definitive assurance of his union with God, Luther had a conception of God that was strongly influenced by the nominalistic theological writers of the fourteenth and fifteenth centuries. This theology emphasized strongly divine liberty and transcendence, but in such a way as to lessen a proper understanding of God's intimate presence to his creatures. In one sense it could be said that the Lutheran God is wholly other than his creation and beyond it, in such a way as to create a tension between the distant and all-holy majesty of the divine and the sinfulness and misery of his human creature. God is thus so exalted above man that he appears to be distant from him; established in solitary majesty, he is characterized by an all-powerful arbitrariness. This distance between God and man is conceived, it seems, almost as one of hostility; in any case, of so total a difference as to lessen a needed and true conception of God's immanence and proximity to his creature.

Catholic thought, and especially the profound theology of St. Thomas Aquinas, had never undervalued the divine transcendence. At the same time it had always kept in balance the immanence and presence to the creature of the transcendent God. If God was the Supreme Being, the principle of all creation and the Lord of heaven, he was also intimately present and operative within man to such an extent that the creature is truly seen as a participation in the being of God. The creature shares in the divine plenitude of being. Even in his natural being and structure he imitates or resembles God. Man is a deficient similitude of the Creator, even in the order of nature apart from the intimacy of participation by supernatural grace. In fact the creature is and has his being only in virtue of his sharing in the being of God.

God: Above and Within

In Catholic theology there is always and necessarily a tension, a dynamic polarity, between the conceptions of the divine transcendence and immanence. If a proper conception of God enables man to keep God's ineffable majesty and supremacy always in view, the fact of an intimate presence and operation of God within the world and the creature is not challenged. *The necessary emphasis on the divine transcendence never becomes an affirmation that God is wholly other, and in some sense set over against man.*

Nor, on the other hand, does an affirmation of God's presence in man and man's participation in God ever degenerate into some sort of pantheistic absorption of the creature into God. There is never any confusion of the divine and the created, which would cause man seemingly to disappear into the divine and be seen merely as a part of and not as a distinct participation in God. Indeed the divine immanence and transcendence are emphasized in such a way as to enhance the distinctiveness and the genuine reality and causality of the creature. The fact of the divine transcendence makes it evident that God is not in any way on the same level of existence with the beings he has created out of nothing. While not opposed to man as wholly other, he is totally distinct from creation and transcends in his majesty the being not only of man but of the whole of creation.

Yet along with this transcendence God is fully immanent to his creation, giving to it reality in being and in activity, creating therefore the immanent reality of man. Man has his being and the genuineness of his action in dependence on God; this, however, only enhances the self-consistency of the creature in his nature and activity, in distinction from yet in participation of God. *God is thus at once wholly beyond man and present in his inmost being; he surpasses the totality of creation yet bestows a genuine reality of creatures and their action.*

God is in no way brought down to the level of the creature, nor is his action on the same level of reality as that of the creature. There can be no doubt that Catholic thought emphasizes the transcendence of the divine majesty. The Fourth Lateran Council (A.D. 1215) approved this forceful and extremely rich sentence: "For between the Creator and the creature no similarity can be found so great but that the dissimilarity is even greater." (D432; *TCT*307) This doctrine, repeated in many formulas of St. Thomas, is a clear statement of the uniqueness of the divine being. Yet at the same time there is similarity and likeness of creation to its Creator. This reality is emphasized in the notion of the immanence and creative presence of God to men. Both are so much a part of the Catholic teaching on God and his action that we must maintain a clear balance and constant tension between the realities of God's transcendence and his immanence. This doctrine, expressed metaphysically and theologically in the whole Thomistic teaching on the *analogy of being*, will form an important aspect of the teaching on grace.

The doctrine of analogy is not an abstract truth of purely philosophic concern, for this doctrine defines the reality of the relationship between God and man. The immanence of God assures the fullest possible reality to man and his action. St. Thomas is able to say that any derogation from the reality and activity of the creature is a derogation of the divine majesty. The intimate presence of God to man, the creative immanence of God, not only assures the full reality and genuine action of the creature, but also forms the basis for a real and personal relationship, through grace, of man with God. Thus the reality of man's relation to God in nature and grace flows from the nature of God and his creative presence to his creature.

Man and Salvation

Implicit in the Lutheran notion of salvation, however, is the tendency previously mentioned to stress God's transcendence at the expense of his immanence and of participation in him by the creature. From the point of view of theology and metaphysics, this has two results of immediate concern. First, the relations of God and man are seen in a more "extrinsecist" fashion, so that God in his majesty and sanctity is not only dissimilar to the creature but, as the God of wrath, is set over against him. Even the God of mercy does not fully restore the intimacy and actuality of the divine action in man. Thus, while Lutheranism stresses the wholly other character of God, it implies a lack of that real relationship and likeness with God which is essential to the Catholic affirmation of him.

Second, the activity of the creature seems to be set at nought, in favor of the exaltation of the divine action. This renders the two more separate, and thereby expresses a view quite different from that of St. Thomas and other traditional Catholic thinkers. In this matter Luther was influenced by a background of nominalistic thought which tended to exalt the Creator in a way derogatory both to God and to the activity of man. It stressed a more extrinsecist theology of man's relation to God. While nominalist theology would tend toward a Pelagian view of man's causality—by conceiving the divine action and transcendence in too external a fashion—Luther would go in the opposite direction. In the order of salvation he would so exalt the divine action as to minimize or even deny the role of man's activity and cooperation with grace. Whereas 53

Catholic thought maintains the necessary interrelationship and tension between the divine transcendence and immanence, and upholds both the divine action and man's cooperation in salvation, Lutheranism like Pelagianism does not maintain this necessary polarity. Unwittingly, the Lutheran theological tradition would destroy both the relation of God to man and the inner harmony of divine and human activity.

Man's Misery

One of the cardinal insights of Luther, in addition to his conception of the divine and human relationship, was a strong sense of the misery, wretchedness, and utter unworthiness before God of sinful man. The Lutheran consciousness of sin was so great that man in his spiritual, religious reality would always remain a sinner—even after the visitation of grace. Human actions and good works might be demanded of the Christian as external obedience to the divine commands, but human actions as such were of no value in the work of justification. They ever remained the works of a totally corrupt nature; they were still the acts of sinful man, even when God imparted forgiveness and justification to him. Lutheran religious consciousness was profoundly aware of the reality of sin. It saw sin where Catholic thought would see rather the weakness of man resulting from sin. When Catholic tradition denied that the goodness of man and his nature was wholly destroyed by sin, either original or personal, Lutheran thought asserted an abiding and complete corruption of nature from any religious point of view. It maintained that grace did not heal human nature and restore it from within, but remained exterior to the depths of man's being. Because of the corruption of nature, man's action could never be elevated to a higher plane of religious reality. It was deemed false by Lutheranism to conceive of grace as a vital power capable of transforming man into a new creature in Christ.

EXTRINSIC JUSTIFICATION   This is the well-known doctrine of the extrinsic imputation of justice. Luther sees justification as merely an external imputing by God to man of the grace and goodness of Christ. Man, meanwhile, inwardly remains a sinner predisposed to evil. Justification changes the person's relationship to God, in this thought system, but in a purely extrinsic way. There is no real change in man, no genuine liberation from sin, the flesh, and death. Sin and sinfulness remain in man always, but for the justified God no longer imputes sin, only righteousness. Without any real, inner transformation, man remains corrupt and sinful. The merits of Christ, however, seem to cloak and cover this evil in man. The God of wrath becomes the God of mercy who no longer considers man in any way except as covered with the mantle of Christ. Grace then is not a divine life bestowed on man, nor a healing light or transforming power. Grace is simply the gracious regard of the God of mercy.

Luther believed that grace was thus an imputation, something extrinsic to man which allowed him to remain the sinful child of Adam. Confusing concupiscence and the desire of sin with sinfulness, or more properly with original sin, Luther denied the reality of transforming grace. What the Christian had was an absolutely certain and profound religious experience giving certitude of justification. This was the moment of faith for Luther—not a faith in divine truth and teaching, but a complete commitment of oneself to Christ, an abandonment to the divine mercy. This was likewise the moment of justification; it brought man the absolute assurance of salvation and acceptance by God through Christ.

ASSURANCE OF SALVATION   Luther, who realized so completely the sinfulness of man, sought the assurance of acceptance before God in spite of sin and evil. In the moment of Lutheran justification, that zenith of religious experience in which man abandons himself in confidence and trust to the divine mercy manifest in Christ, this assurance is given. The justified man has experienced the divine mercy. His faith is a confidence in the salvation of God. Justification is not a reality in him but an extrinsic matter, yet man is possessed of a full confidence in salvation. This supreme religious moment, for Luther, is purely individual. There is no question of entering into a relation with God by an entrance into the mystical body, the Church, for Luther will deny the profound and sacramental reality of the Church in the Catholic sense. What is essential is the individual aware of his incapacity for God, accepting the message of Christ, abandoning himself to Jesus in a unique, trusting act which assures him of his salvation.

FREEDOM   Man's free will is denied its freedom in this outlook, for man is dominated by God (or by sin) in such a way that it is God alone who *acts* to save him. The impotence of free will is one aspect of Luther's mode of conceiving the *total* causality of God. In the process of salvation, God alone acts. He induces no internal change in the creature, and never renders man capable of acting in grace. Paradoxically, this assertion of the powerlessness of freedom leads to an exaltation of

55

individualism. Lutheranism comes to be characterized by a building up of the individual at the expense of the Church. It involves a denial of the Church and its role in salvation as understood throughout Catholic tradition. Thus, Lutheran thought denies the power of freedom, and at the same time attributes salvation to the *sole* and total causality of God. His action *replaces* or substitutes itself for that of the creature. In the moment of justification by God, an act entirely unrelated to the Church, man receives an absolute assurance of his salvation directly from God. The individual is emancipated completely, in the Lutheran view, from all creatures in the order of salvation. Lutheranism thus appears to be a champion of individual religious liberty. This liberty can only be seen as ultimately unreal, however, if God's creative presence and immanence to man does not really transform him from within and bestow on him healing grace—the power to act freely and well.

A View of Lutheranism

Lutheranism is a religious system at variance with Catholicity on many points. Basically, it challenges the whole range of Catholic understanding of man's relationship with God. The far-reaching consequences of Luther's teaching called forth the pronouncements of the Council of Trent, in which the Church reaffirmed the Catholic teaching on grace and salvation. The position of the Church was centered around several aspects of Christian doctrine: the Lutheran understanding of original sin and its consequences, implying a total corruption of man's nature and the impotence of his will; the conception of grace and justification as merely external actions of God which do not affect man in his depths nor transform him from within; the Lutheran notion of justifying faith as a moment of confiding abandon to Christ, which gives assurance of salvation.

THE COUNCIL OF TRENT

Catholic doctrine on these questions, formulated in opposition to Lutheranism, was presented in full at the Council of Trent, as it had been previously by Pope Leo X in the Bull *"Exsurge Domine"* of June 15, 1520. The teaching of Trent centers on two points of fundamental importance for the understanding of the Catholic doctrine on grace. First of all, *justification is a real and profound transformation of man, a genuine gift of sanctification to him.* It can in no way be reduced to

56

something purely external. Second, *man is not deprived of freedom, but cooperates through grace in justification and the process of salvation.* Justification is not solely the action of God, in other words, but a process in which man participates. We may follow the order of the Council in expressing these doctrines.

The reality of the effects of original sin is that "all men had lost innocence in the sin of Adam" (D793; *TCT*557); this means that all are "born without justice." (D795; *TCT*559) That does not, however, connote a total corruption of men, for "their free will, though weakened and unsteady, was by no means destroyed." (*Ibid.*) Sinful man is estranged from God and unable to attain salvation except through Christ, for it is only in Christ that we "might secure justice and that all might receive the adoption of sons." (D794; *TCT*558)

We may note the Council's insistence on a genuine securing of justice by man, thus stressing the reality of the divine gift of grace. This redemption by Christ, the only means of salvation for man, comprises a genuine transformation. "So, likewise, they [men] would never have been justified except through rebirth in Christ, for this rebirth bestows on them, through the merit of his passion, the grace by which they are justified." (D795; *TCT*559) These solemn declarations reaffirm Catholic faith in opposition to Lutheranism, as well as to any revived Pelagian spirit (cf. D811f; *TCT*575f.) Man cannot save himself but is saved only in the transforming grace of Christ. A brief definition is then proposed: "Justification is a passing from the state in which man is born a son of the first Adam, to the state of grace and *adoption as sons* [Rom 8,15] of God through the Second Adam, Jesus Christ our Savior." (D796; *TCT*560) The Council immediately adds that this transformation demands baptism or at least the desire of baptism, thus affirming in the very heart of the work of salvation the basic principle of sacramentality.

Human Cooperation

In direct opposition to the Reformation theology of the sole agency of God, the Council solemnly proclaims the need for the adult to co-operate with grace by his free will. Although man "could not take one step toward justice in God's sight" without grace, he responds to the divine initiative by "freely consenting to it and cooperating with that grace." (D797; *TCT*561) It is clear, then, that divine action and grace do not destroy man's action or render it unnecessary. The Council solemnly condemns the real inertness of man in Lutheran thought: "If anyone says that the free will of man, moved and awakened by God, in no way cooperates with the awakening call of God by an assent by which man disposes and prepares himself to receive the grace of justification; or says that man cannot dissent, if he wishes, but *like an object without life,* does nothing at all and is merely passive; let him be anathema." (D814; *TCT*578; cf. D815f; *TCT*579f.)

Man is redeemed only in Christ's grace. God's initiative is always asserted, but it is not an initiative which takes away man's response; rather, the reality of God's gracious call and bestowal of grace demands the reality of man's deep, personal, and free cooperation. It is essential to see that Catholic doctrine, unlike the extremes of Pelagianism and Lutheranism, never sets up an either/or understanding of the reality of God's grace and man's cooperation. The very assertion for the Catholic of the primacy of God's mercy and grace is completed by the affirmation of man's cooperation and genuine human activity in the work of salvation.

The necessity and even the psychology of man's cooperation are expressed in a long passage which is a cogent summary of traditional Catholic teaching. God's summons of man to salvation is not man's work, but the free initiative of God; to it man assents, or from it he turns away. For the man who gives his free assent there is a passage from faith— not a mere confidence in the Lutheran sense but an assent to divine revelation—through sorrow and repentance for sin, to hope in God's mercy. On the basis of an initial love and in a spirit of sorrow for evil done, man seeks baptism and desires to begin a "new life" in Christ. (D797f; *TCT*561f) Clearly the reality of grace demands the reality of man's cooperation. The latter in no way minimizes but properly exalts the love and mercy of God. From his first step to God to the last moment of life, man truly acts in the order of salvation, under grace. This description of coming to justification may be compared with the earlier affirmations, in the same divine tradition, of the councils that opposed Pelagianism. The Council of Trent, after this statement, comes to one of its most celebrated definitions.

Justification

In a clear, religiously profound statement the Council defines the inner nature and structure of justification. It does so in direct opposition to the extrinsecist position of Reformation theology. The heart of Catholic teaching is contained in this passage. First of all comes the assertion that *"justification is not only the remission of sins, but* sanctification *and* renovation *of the interior man through the voluntary reception of grace and the gifts, whereby man becomes* just *instead of* unjust, *a friend instead of an enemy, that he may be an heir in the hope of life everlasting."* The Council then details the causes of this inner transformation: *its goal and purpose is God's glory; it is brought about by God through the merits of our Redeemer, and communicated to man in faith and baptism.*

Trent's Idea of Grace

As part of the Lutheran views of salvation, of the corruption of medieval thought, the Council states:

> The unique formal cause is the justice of God, not the justice by which he is himself just, but the justice by which he makes us just, namely, the justice which we *have* as a gift from him and by which we are renewed in the spirit of our mind. Not only are we considered just, but we are truly said to be just, and we are just, each one of us receiving *within* himself his own justice, according as the measure of the Holy Spirit imparts to each one as he wishes, and according to the disposition and cooperation of each. (D799; TCT563)

In the solemn words of a condemnation, the Council rejects the notion that this grace is "through the imputation of Christ's justice alone" (D821; TCT585; cf. D820; TCT584.) Without giving a detailed theological explanation of formal causality, the Council affirms that the inner structure of the justification of man is not something identical with God or Christ, but is a gift bestowed by God in Christ by which man is made just; it is something proper to man transformed in Christ.

The whole Catholic theology of grace as a created reality, distinct from God himself, and bestowed upon man as something personal to him is here stated by the Council. Furthermore, this justice within man *inheres* within him as a permanent principle: "The charity of God is poured forth by the Holy Spirit into the hearts of those who are justified and *inheres* in them." (D800; TCT564) Again, in the words of a definitive condemnation: "If anyone says that men are justified . . . excluding *grace* and charity which is poured forth in their hearts by the Holy Spirit and *inheres* in them . . . let him be anathema." (D821; TCT585) What theology calls "sanctifying grace" is here determined and defined as opposite to the Lutheran teaching of a kind of justification which does not inwardly transform man but remains extrinsic to him. The Church solemnly affirms the inner reality of grace as a principle inhering within each individual who is sanctified by God. It is the very reality of God's action that implies the reality within man which is grace and justice.

GRACE AND SIN   This justification involves negatively the remission of sins. Positively it means transformation into a new life in Christ. "Whence in the very act of being justified, at the same time that his sins are remitted, a man receives through Jesus Christ, to whom he is joined, the infused gifts of faith, hope and charity." (D800; *TCT*564) In other words, *justification is both a destruction of sin and a union with Christ which effects the communication of a life expressed in the virtues of faith, hope, and charity.* This latter point is developed by the Council to contradict the Lutheran position of justification through trustful faith alone: "For faith without hope and charity neither perfectly unites a man with Christ nor makes him a living member of his body." (*Ibid.*)

Faith

Faith is, indeed, the beginning and the continuing foundation of new life in Christ, but it is the faith of the Church and not Luther's absolute confidence in personal salvation. This point is expressly made by the Council, which states that, "no one can know with the certitude of faith admitting no error, that he has obtained God's grace" (D802; *TCT*566); or again: "If anyone says that man is absolved from his sins and justified because he believes with certainty that he is absolved and justified . . . let him be anathema." (D824; *TCT*588; cf. D823; *TCT*587.) The Council thus solemnly excludes the Lutheran error of absolute faith in one's personal salvation, thereby rejecting both the individualism of this view and, specifically, the attempt to base justification on the inner subjective certitude of a private religious experience. The Council here does not condemn a reasoned and reasonable estimation of one's personal state of grace but wishes to make two central points. The first is to deny the founding of a hope of salvation on the subjective experience of the individual and his feelings: the self-assertion of Lutheran "interior religion" is condemned. Second, the Council, with Sacred Scripture, centers the Christian's hope and assurance not in man's personal states but in the divine efficacy of Christ's redemption and sacraments: "For no devout man should entertain doubts about God's mercy, Christ's merits, and the power and efficacy of the sacraments." 60 (D802; *TCT*566) It might be said that in the latter connection the Church is reaffirming the words of St. Paul: "For in hope were we saved"

(Rom 8,24), thereby establishing the faith and hope of the Christian in God and Christ, and not in man and his experiences no matter how profound or religious.

Growth In Grace

Further indication of the reality of the inner gift of grace is the declaration of the Council that man may grow in justice. We are therefore to admit degrees of justification which vary according to the gift of God and man's dispositions and cooperation with grace. The justified man can advance "from virtue to virtue, renewed day by day" by good works; "the justified increase in the very justice they have received through the grace of Christ, and are justified the more." (D803; TCT567) Indeed, the good works of the justified man are not mere signs of his religious conversion. Being done in grace, they are themselves the causes of an increase in the degree and reality of man's sanctification. (D834; TCT598) The whole moral life of the Christian is the expression of the inner life of grace. Doing what is good is made possible by the power of grace. Although venial sin cannot be fully avoided, the justified man is capable of pursuing a life of goodness. The power to do so comes from grace. Besides the root power there is the inner drive of the life of grace, which naturally expresses itself in good action. So true is this that the Council affirms: "God 'does not abandon' those who have been justified by his grace, 'unless they abandon him first.'" (D804; TCT568)

From its genesis at the beginning of man's life to its consummation at the end, the work of man's salvation is inseparably the gratuitous gift of God and the free cooperation of man. Having affirmed this of man's preparation for justification, of the moment of justification itself, and of the whole life of the justified man, the Council also affirms this truth with regard to man's perseverance to the last moment of life. "If anyone says that without God's special help it is possible for a justified man to persevere in the justice he has received, or says that with God's special help it is impossible, let him be anathema." (D832; TCT596; cf. D806; TCT570.) The consummation of man's life in the act of death—the final and decisive moment of earthly existence—is an act of salvation and justice in virtue of the grace of God. In a sense, the whole life of grace prepares for this crucial moment. In it the justified man turns to God to consecrate his life to him by dying in Christ. This moment is one of cooperation with the divine liberality. It is at the same time a moment 61 of man's cooperation with divine love.

Merit

As part of the Lutheran views of salvation, of the corruption of man's nature and freedom, and of the extrinsecism of justification, there came a denial of the traditional Catholic doctrine of merit. Against this conclusion of Reformation theology the Council of Trent reasserted the reality of merit through grace, indicating again thereby the reality of man's action in the order of salvation. Because of his union with Christ in grace, man is enabled to work for his own eternal beatitude. He merits heaven by the power of grace and his free cooperation in performing good works.

> Eternal life should be set before those who persevere in good works to the end and who hope in God. It should be set before them as being the grace that God, through Jesus Christ, has mercifully promised his sons . . . and as the reward which, according to the promise of God himself, must assuredly be given them for their good works and merits. (D809; TCT573)

It is because of God's creative love for man that he promises to reward the merit of man's good works. It is a proof of the efficacious reality of that love that human actions attain this high value before God.

> Although in Holy Scripture high value is placed on good works [Mt 10,42] . . . nevertheless a Christian should have no inclination to rely on himself or to glory in himself instead of the Lord [cf. 1 Cor 1,31; 2 Cor 10,17], whose goodness toward all men is such that he wants his gifts to be their merits. (D810; TCT574)

The work of man's salvation is invariably the work of God's grace, but the affirmation of the reality of grace necessarily involves, in Catholic thought, the corresponding affirmation of man's free cooperation. This cooperation is not a mere passive openness or receptivity; it is an active engagement in the life of justice and righteousness. The reality of this human activity is affirmed not only in its immediacy in this world but in its effects before God himself.

The doctrine of merit is a fitting way to conclude the treatment of the Council of Trent, for merit comes as a crown to man's acts. *This is not to imply that merit is an extrinsic reward, a sort of present given by God for good behavior.* The doctrine of merit is not added to the doc-

62

trine of man's inner cooperation with grace as an afterthought. It is merely the definition of a property or quality inherent in the good works of grace, and demonstrates very clearly the totality of the Catholic affirmation of grace. Merit is not in any sense an arbitrary aspect of the good act. It is proof that in the good act man disposes himself before God, and that the reality of good works is of more than merely passing and terrestrial importance.

The doctrine of the Council is found in summary form in this condemnatory statement:

> If anyone says that the good works of a justified man are gifts of God to such an extent that they are not also the merits of the justified man himself; or that, by the good works he performs through the grace of God and the merits of Jesus Christ (of whom he is a living member), the justified man does not truly merit an increase of grace, life everlasting and, provided that he dies in the state of grace, the attainment of that life everlasting, and even an increase of glory, let him be anathema. (D842; *TCT*606)

This is the essential Catholic teaching on the reality of merit. The first part of the condemnation is a direct refutation of a fundamental Reformation intuition: that God's action in justification and salvation really removes all genuine and intrinsic human cooperation with grace. The Council reaffirms the Catholic doctrine—which, as mentioned, is always a simultaneous affirmation of the reality of the divine causality and that of man. Because good works of the supernatural order are done with the aid of grace from beginning to end, it does not mean in any way that the reality of man's causality is diminished. Grace does not disregard or do away with human freedom. It heals it from within, so that man is able to perform freely and meritoriously good acts which are his.

Finally, the Council teaches that man, in this life, merits an increase of grace. This, of course, is not a quantitative matter but a question of both intensity and the deep-rootedness of grace in the very being of the justified man. In traditional theological terms, the state of grace is qualitatively intensified. This means that man is more closely assimilated to Christ with whom he is united. Looking to the final destiny of man, the Council affirms that good works performed in this life are meritorious of everlasting life in heaven; there man's assimilation to Christ will be complete, there the life of grace will find its inner and total development.

63

Conclusion

Man had been set free from God by Pelagianism to work out his own salvation on his own strength, independently of any genuine and healing internal grace. The heresy denied essential teaching on the reality of original sin and its effects, and considered sinful man as capable of all goodness necessary for salvation; it was, in brief, a naturalistic denial of the need for grace. It rested on a false conception of man and his freedom, as if he were emancipated from God. The role of God and his grace in the order of salvation was minimized. Justification, good works, and merit were seen as the results of man's *sole agency*. Man, basically, was the agent in human salvation. The agency or causality of God and grace was denied.

From this point of view, Lutheranism represents the opposite extreme. The reality of original sin and its effects were maximized; man's nature and capacity for action in the order of salvation were denied or considered impotent. This radical incapacity of man was made up for by the *sole agency* of God, who is active in the process of justification without causing in man the reality of healing and elevating grace. This was a supernaturalism which was derogatory both to the reality of God's action and to human causality and freedom. God's action by grace is appreciated fully only when we profess, with the Council of Trent, that his grace is so real and so genuinely efficacious that it is able to transform sinful man into justified man through remission from sin and the bestowal of an interior gift.

The Council of Trent likewise denied the epistemological dimension of the Lutheran affirmation of God's agency; that is to say, Luther's understanding of God's action in justification was such as to reverberate in human consciousness by an absolute inner certitude of personal salvation. Denying the *basis* for this view of God's action, the Council likewise denied its *translation into the sphere of conscious knowledge*: that is, its epistemological dimension. The certitude and hope of the Christian are to rest in God and in the power of his works. By thus relating grace and justification to the works and sacraments of the Church, the Council denied the isolated individualism of Lutheran salvation, and reaffirmed salvation's sacramental and ecclesial character. Grace comes to man through Christ in the Church, that is in the power of the Spirit and in the sacraments of faith. Grace makes man therefore a living member of Christ in his mystical body.

The agency of either man or God as the sole one in man's salvation, i.e., the either/or position of the extremes of Pelagianism and Lutheranism is thus denied by the Church. Catholic doctrine assents to the reality and to the absolute primacy and sovereignty of God's grace. In that very assertion it simultaneously affirms the reality of man's free cooperation, made possible by the totally gratuitous gift of healing and elevating grace.

Note: See Appendix for the teachings of Baius, Jansenius, and Pascal.

CHAPTER THREE

SUMMARY OF THE THEOLOGY OF GRACE

NATURE AND GRACE

St. John has indicated the basic truth of the whole theology of grace. It is the desire of the Father to communicate his love to man, which is essentially a giving of himself and his life to his human creatures. God creates a being capable of receiving this divine gift of love, a creature able to enter into personal relationship with his Creator. Ultimately this gift is the final perfect union of man with God in heaven—his immediate vision of God, and definitive entering into the very beatitude and glory of the blessed Trinity. Most radically then, what God's love wills for man is God himself, a communication not only of divine gifts which are less than God, but the giving of himself in an eternal union by which man in heaven enters into the life of the Trinity in a way totally beyond anything that could come to man *as a creature.*

The whole of Catholic thought on the reality of grace rests on the principle that the gift of God himself is totally beyond the capacities and demands of what man the creature is. The life of the triune God is absolutely and necessarily supernatural with respect to angels and men: that is, absolutely proper to and distinctive of God himself, in that which distinguishes him from all other realities. Yet it is the personal life of God which, in love, he wishes to share with man; it is not merely being or reality or existence which God wills to give man but his own life, his own existence, his own personal love. This he wishes to communicate. We have seen this communication spoken of in the New Testament with a rich abundance of thought and language. God wishes to incorporate man into his Son, to transform man through friendship with himself.

Man's Destiny

The destiny of man is then to enter into a genuine friendship with the personal God, to know and love him as he is. The whole of Christian thought revolves around this love of God. The essence of true love and friendship is that it be free—on both sides. Thus, God is sovereignly free in the communication of himself, but man must also be free. He must be free as a person and as a creature in order to receive and respond to the initiative of divine love. Any genuine understanding or experience of personal love reveals its free character, for persons can respond to each other in love only when there is mutual freedom.

Freedom is necessary, for love is the mutual giving and receiving of what is most personal and distinctive. The love of a person must be given freely, to another person capable of a free response. The very notion of gift which is at the heart of love is its quality of being a free bestowal, a largesse, an undemanded generosity. The gift of love means a gratuitous generosity, but it is complemented by a receiving which is in the order of free response, hence true human love. The more profound the love the greater is its freedom, so that the most exalted possible free gift is that of the person in his most intimate reality.

God's Love

In the supernatural order, there is manifested the most absolute giving in totally gratuitous love. The transcendent God, who is the fullness of reality and the plenitude of all being, is supremely free. Above all, he is free in the communication of what is most truly and profoundly his: his personal being in the Father, Son, and Spirit. Man cannot have an adequate conception of God's freedom, but some notion of its absolute character is to be gained by considering that God's love is so ultimately free that it creates the very objects of his love. The noblest and highest human love is always a response to the goodness and value of the person who is the object of love. But God's love is never a response to something or someone existing apart from him. God's love *creates* whom and what it loves, and thus in supreme gratuity gives reality itself to the object of his love.

Man is constituted in his very being by the creative love of God, so that he is totally dependent on the power of the Creator both as to his coming into being and his continuance in being. In other words, both the consistency and reality of man, as well as his activity, depend upon God. This does not imply that man and his action are less real, but rather guarantees the actuality of the creation. The dependence of man upon the Creator is the cause of the genuine consistency, i.e. the true being, of man. God who is the absolute plenitude of all reality transcends the creature wholly as the real and distinct principle of all created reality.

In order to enter into personal relations with man, God creates him as a being who is capable of genuine action and response in his own right. To insure the reality of the creature's role in his ultimate destiny, God must make the creature in such a way that he will be able to respond to him in a real and personal action of his own. Man, therefore, must have within him the dynamic capabilities of true action. He must exist in such a way that his actions are his own, and not merely a divine action taking place within him. A proper understanding of the reality of creation implies not only the distinction of Creator and creature but also the inner realism of the creature and his capacity for true action in knowledge and love.

The Reality of Man

68   The divine desire to communicate with a personal creature necessitates in man a being who truly exists, and who acts with integrity. Only

in this way is it possible to maintain the reality of his response to creative love. God creates a being who with his own resources of action can respond to him in knowledge and love. *Only a person can respond to a person; only personal love can answer to personal love.* The divine intention of entering into personal relations with a creature presupposes the reality of the creature's capability of love and action. This means the constitution of a creature with a definite nature and being of his own. Man is thus created as a personal incarnate spirit with his own proper natural consistency and with the fundamental capacities to know and to love. He exists as a being who is radically able by his personal actions to respond to the gift of divine love and grace.

Nature and Supernature

Grace presupposes nature, we say, because only with a true rational nature can man act toward God. Only with his own real capacity of action can man enter into a real friendship with him. *The life of grace means precisely entering into friendship with the divine persons, and this means being able to receive the gift of God's love with full awareness and knowledge of the absolute freedom and gratuity of the gift.* God's self-giving in grace is certainly gratuitous, and thus truly a love on his part. It must be received in the same way by the creature, man. He must be able to recognize God's love as a gift, and must be able to respond to him freely and in love, that is, as a person.

If man, then, must be a personal spirit able to exist and act on the foundation of a natural structure and reality, he must also be open to the personal invitation of God's love. He must have a capacity for the infinite; he must be a being not closed in upon himself but able to go out in knowledge and love to a personal encounter with the personal God. The natures of created beings lesser than man are not open in this way to God, for lower creatures cannot transcend themselves; they are enclosed, in a sense, in their own natural being. But by his nature, man is capable of going out of himself to meet God. He is created in such a way as to be able to enter into relationship with the divine persons. Not only is man capable of this in an absolute sense; he is so constituted that he can welcome God in virtue of his own deepest longings and desires.

Gratuitous Grace

This does not mean in any sense that man's natural structure or dynamism of action demands the personal gift of divine love. Precisely

69

the opposite holds true, for man in his nature and activity must be capable of receiving God's gift as totally gratuitous. This means that man's nature must be so genuinely self-consistent in its constitution so that it does not demand grace by any sort of natural necessity. Rather the inner reality of nature must be such as to allow man to be truly man, and thus to be capable of responding to God's love freely and without any inner exigency or compulsion. Catholic theology, in maintaining this position, respects not only the genuine being of man but also the gratuity and supernatural character of the divine personal gift. The very transcendence of the gift demands the reality of nature, which is to say that the proper appreciation of the order of grace involves an accurate view of the structure of nature.

If, then, human nature does not *demand* grace, it is yet open to grace, and this in a unique way not shared by any work of creation below it. This openness is shown in the capacity of man for a knowledge of the reality of being and in his ability to love reality as good. Man's abilities to know and to love find their proper field of exercise in the world of created beings, but in their activity they manifest the power to go beyond the individual realities of this world. Man can come to know the principle and source of all things in the world. Human love, too, can never be fully satisfied with the goodness of individual creatures.

Man's powers of knowledge and love thus manifest a capacity which is not limited by this world. For this reason the gift of God himself can be received by man and welcomed as the ultimate and absolute fulfill-ment of his deepest longings. Man is constituted in such a way as to be truly a self-consistent being, but at the same time he is a personal spirit capable of being elevated to the order of grace. He can receive the gift of God as the ultimate perfection of his nature and as the gratuitous beneficence of divine love, a reality wholly beyond the demands and expectations of his nature.

SANCTIFYING GRACE

Introduction

God's will to give himself to man is realized in its ultimate form in man's vision and possession of God in heaven. This destiny is at the same time God's gift and the final consummation of a life of cooperation with grace on earth. *Indeed the life of grace is at once the receiving by man of God himself and the inner transformation which elevates man's nature so as to render it capable of union with God.* If God's gift of him-

70

self is *uncreated grace,* then *created grace* is that which enables man to be and to act in terms of the divine gift and his own supernatural destiny. St. Thomas speaks of uncreated grace primarily in the theology of the *missions* of the persons of the blessed Trinity. (*S.Th.,* 1ª, 43) So, too, we shall leave the primary consideration of uncreated grace and the divine indwelling to the theology of the Trinity and concentrate on the theology of created grace. However, it is always to be kept in mind that the reality of created grace is to be understood in reference to that grace which is God himself. The theology of created grace, therefore, will be constantly related to the Trinity, and to the work of redemption accomplished in Christ and carried on through the Church sacramentally in the Holy Spirit.

The Supernatural

With grace theology associates in a special way the concept of the *supernatural.* In this context the supernatural means that which is essentially gratuitous: a gift of God which is not demanded or required for the inner consistency or integrity of man's natural structure and activity. The supernatural is something above, in excess of, nature, and it therefore remains intrinsically gratuitous. The reason for this transcendence of grace is its intimate relationship with the absolutely transcendent reality of the inner life of the divine persons. God's communication of being and reality constitutes the natural order of creation. *His communication of himself in his own personal life constitutes the supernatural order of grace.* This order is uniquely *gratuitous* and thus has the real character of *excess* with regard to the order of creation.

Created grace is bestowed on man so that he may respond as a person to God's personal gift. Grace makes man capable of supernatural action by elevating him in his whole being to a new life. Because man is to live and act in a new way which is truly his own, internal grace corresponds to the distinction in man of nature and activity. Grace is given, in other words, to elevate man's nature and powers of action as well as to elevate his actions themselves. Theology distinguishes between *habitual* and *actual* grace. Habitual grace is that which is given as a *new nature* to man. Because of the work it does it is termed *sanctifying* grace. As an abiding and qualitative elevation of his *powers of action,* habitual grace can mean the gift of the supernatural *virtues.*

The *possibility of individual acts* in the supernatural order (as contrasted with a habitual power), is the result of gifts of *actual* graces.

The Nature of Sanctifying Grace

Sanctifying grace is something created which inheres in the soul as the real result of God's love. (Cf. S.Th., 1ª,20,2.) It is not simply an effect caused by God in a transient fashion, but a quality which man is given as a continuing result or abiding consequence of God's love. St. Thomas sees the divine mercy providing for man in so real a manner that a new form of being is bestowed on him, a new nature in a sense, which qualifies his deepest being. From the moment of justification, God infuses into man's nature a new quality which is the abiding principle of union with him and the source of all supernatural activity in the state of grace.

Sanctifying grace is understood to be a quality which is possessed in the very structure of man's reality. Grace is not itself the substantial reality of man's being, nor is it the substance of God—although created grace relates to the special presence of God. Even if it is not man's being, it is yet a true reality. *It may be seen then as a quality which inheres in man as truly bestowed on him, as a qualitative possession which man has and which possesses man.* Sanctifying grace is considered to be a *habitus.* The word means primarily, in the present context, an abiding disposition of the whole man, a created entity elevating him to a special life in relation to God. To say that grace is considered a *habitus* is to state in formal terms that the reality of the new life bestowed on the Christian is something which truly and inwardly affects his being. It emphasizes that grace is present as a new nature, that is, as a permanent source of new life. This *habitus* is further called *entitative* rather than operative, in order to stress the fact that the whole of man in his deepest *being* is qualified and disposed by grace. The phrase *state of grace* refers directly to the reality of sanctifying grace. It emphasizes that this new life in Christ is truly given to man, and truly inheres in his soul.

A Created Gift

As a created gift, grace is finite; it is given to man in varying degrees of intensity. Grace is capable of becoming more intense, of taking hold of man in a more profound way. This dynamic reality is a new being and a new life because it is a participation in the being of God in his own reality. This finite, created gift of God is thus immediately related to the infinite, being at once a created reality and a sharing in the uncreated life of the Trinity. This is not to say that grace

72

is a *part* of the divine life in any quantitative or pantheistic sense. Rather, grace is a created reality in its metaphysical structure, but in so unique a way as to be an immediate sharing in what is infinite—God in his own being. This is precisely the point of mystery at which human understanding reaches its limit. Created grace is at once both finite and intentionally—that is, in its power and tendency—infinite. Why infinite? Because it gives a participation in that life which God is. Created grace is not identified with God, but it is intrinsically supernatural because of its direct communion with the divine being.

A Participation in the Divine

Theology seeks to state this mystery in more precise terms by saying that sanctifying grace is a *formal* and *physical* participation in that being and nature which is uniquely divine and proper to God himself. Grace is neither a moral imitation of God or his attributes nor merely a created sharing in the divine activity. Any created reality is a participation in being, the ultimate perfection of which is realized in the absolute being; but grace is more than this for it is a formal sharing in the nature of God, the Absolute. God becomes the "form" or determining principle of the being and operation of the nature that is "graced." The participation in God is physical in the sense that it is achieved by means of a created reality *physically* and really inhering in the soul; a sharing in the divine nature is the result. *Morally* we imitate God or participate in Him by acts of love or knowledge. This distinctive moral participation is rooted in the reality of sanctifying grace. The latter, being a new nature, is the vital source of supernatural actions. The phrase *physical participation,* on the other hand, is used to indicate the inherent "physical" reality of the gift of created grace, which is a formal participation in the divine reality.

When grace is termed a "formal participation in the divine nature," our understanding of God's nature as the source of divine knowledge and love is implied. Although we know that in God being and activity are identical, it is permissible to conceive of a divine nature which "grounds" the divine actions and is the source of God's operation. Specifically, those personal and beatifying actions of God which are his knowledge and love are seen as rooted in the divine nature. It is in the divine nature so understood that grace participates, for grace is a new nature which is the source and principle of actions (faith, hope, charity), themselves a sharing in divine knowledge and love.

Grace, the root and ground of supernatural, divine activity, is a

73

participation in the divine nature seen as the principle of God's own actions. The word *formal* means that grace gives man a participation in that which is proper and specific to the divine nature.

In other words, formal participation is a share in what is uniquely and distinctively God's. Here again is the mystery of grace, for grace is something created, limited, yet at the same time it is formally and really what it is by being properly a sharing in what is divine. What God himself is in his own nature and in an infinite, uncreated way, he gives to man in a way which is finite and limited. Man is given by sanctifying grace a participation in what is truly divine. This is formal participation, yet because a finite realization and a created reality are involved, it must be that this formal participation exists in a *manner* different from its existence in God. *The physical and formal participation in the reality of the divine nature is therefore something realized within the soul of the Christian by way of analogy.*

Grace and Participation

It is inherent in the notion of creation that all creatures are participations of God because each creature shares in being and imitates, in some way, the divine perfections. Yet this is not a *formal* participation in the divine nature, for it is not a sharing in what is unique and specific to God himself. Indeed, both man and God are beings but they are not formally the same *as* beings. The reality of God is absolute existence subsistent in itself, whereas the reality of man is not that he is existence but that he is man, that is, a determined type of existing being. That existence which is God is wholly and absolutely existence: the pure act of existing, the unique being who is the ultimate perfection of all beings and of their reality. This is proper (or formal) and specific with regard to God alone.

Creatures, however, while they are also existences, are determined to being and existing as specific and determined "units" of existence. The very being of God is to be—totally and absolutely; the being of man, however, is to be man, not simply to be. Together with all creatures, man participates in being as an effect of God's creation. By creation he receives a being, a nature, which has its own proper structure and thus its own limited, specific existence. But this being is not a formal participation in what is truly and properly the divine nature. Man's being is to be a man, and God is not a man. Man's being is not then formally the same as God's being, although his whole reality is dependent upon God. By creation man shares in being in a way proper to him, and not formally proper to God. By grace, however, man is given to share, in a created way, that which is specifically and formally God's. Created grace is what it specifically is by being properly and formally a sharing in the divine nature.

The statement developed at length above, that grace is a *habitus*, a created, qualitative reality truly inhering in the soul, thus receives its true meaning and formal significance from the fact that it is a formal participation in the divine nature.

ASPECTS OF GRACE

Adoptive Sonship

The theological doctrine just outlined seeks to illuminate the truth of the radical transformation of man by grace which has been previously examined in the New Testament and in the declarations of the Council of Trent. Theology also seeks to state how it is that man by grace becomes a son of God in receiving the adoption of sonship in Christ, of which St. Paul spoke. Christ himself is the unique Son of the Father by nature. Christ possesses, or rather is, the divine essence or nature, and is thus of the same nature as the Father. Yet the Christian receives sanctifying grace as a true and formal participation of the divine nature. *This communicated reception of the divine nature makes the Christian in a true and real sense a son of God.* Being a child of God means being directly in a new relation to God. God is not only the Creator. He becomes in a special way the term of a relationship which has as its foundation real participation in his (divine) nature.

CREATION AND GRACE Creation endows man with a nature that is distinctively human. This nature of his, as we have noted, does not cause him to share formally in what is properly the divine nature. In that sense, he is not by nature a child of God. The bestowal of sanctifying grace, however, is truly a regeneration and a rebirth; it is a new birth in the power of the Spirit, by which man receives in the literal and formal sense a sharing in the nature which is uniquely God's.

This is man's adoption into divine sonship. It is an adoption because the gift of grace is received by a human person already constituted in his proper nature, who thus receives grace as a new nature. What this divine sonship consists in is a relation to God whereby man is adopted into a new life and a new sphere of activity which centers immediately upon God himself. The blessed Trinity—the foundation and basis of this 75 new relationship—is the ultimate reality of the nature new in grace: the sharing by man in the divine nature.

FAITH AND CHARITY   As a son of God, man is made capable of actions which are direct participations in the actions of God. By faith and charity man shares in God's knowledge and love. His most important acts as a Christian are those he is made capable of by the gift of grace. Being a son of God, man is capable of attaining the destiny of his new inheritance. With his adoption as son, man comes into an anticipated possession of the eternal inheritance of heaven. This inheritance will be the total beatitude and ultimate perfection that comes with the vision of God. Grace is a reflection in this life of the bliss of the life of heaven. Indeed, St. Thomas assures us that that grace which is bestowed on earth remains specifically the same in heaven. Grace is the seed of glory, the inchoative and anticipated foundation of the new life which will be perfected in eternity. (Cf. S.Th., 1ª2ᵃᵉ,111,3, ad 2; 2ª2ᵃᵉ,24,3, ad 2.) The Christian is truly the adopted son of God in virtue of a formal participation in the divine nature. As a new nature, grace is the source of a new life. This life is defined in terms of the primary divine activities in man, of faith and charity. By grace, then, man attains to God even in this life. But the inner completion of this life, begun in reality with the possession of sanctifying grace, will be that inheritance of sons which is ultimate union with God in the knowledge and love of heaven.

Indwelling Presence

The supernatural knowledge and love which are the expressions-in-act of man's new nature are the signs of the life of grace. Man is endowed with this new principle of action that he may be able to attain God immediately as the form and object of living faith and charity. Activity is that perfection of nature which is a principle of action ordered to operation. Operation in turn is the perfection of grace, in the sense that the activities of grace attain to God directly by uniting man, in knowledge and love, to the divine persons. As a new principle of vital action, grace brings with it the gifts of faith and charity. God as he is in a Trinity of persons may be present to the soul in grace in a wholly new way. The very structure of the life of grace, faith, and love is a representation of the divine Trinity. It is an imitation within man of the divine persons. The structure of grace is not only an effect of the divine power but also a likeness of the divine exemplar—an imitation of the life of the divine Trinity. (Cf. S.C.G., 4,21.)

76

NEW PRESENCE   God is present to the creature in a new way in the sense that a new exercise and effect of the divine activity is denoted by grace. *The full uniqueness of the life of grace is realized in the order of operation in which God is available to man as the very object of his knowledge and love.* The living image of the Trinity develops in the order of action: of the virtues of faith and charity and their activity. (*S.Th.*, 1ª,93,7) The presence of the divine persons is realized in the habitual knowledge and love given with the virtues of faith and charity. It is realized fully in the actual operation of these virtues.

The indwelling presence of the divine persons, spoken of clearly in St. John's gospel, is realized in the first infusion of grace and the virtues, when God becomes newly present as the immediate object of knowledge and love. (*S.Th.*, 1ª,43,3 and 5) God thus enters internally and intrinsically into the operation of man. Man is united to God as God is, in the depths of the trinitarian life. The whole life of man, and indeed the whole history of the world, reaches its culminating moment in these divine-human acts which attain to the divine persons and thus manifest the glorious life of the Trinity. The objective presence of God (that is, as object) by grace, and its dynamic expression in faith and love, is something new and unique. It gives to the Christian the divine being in the three persons. This is a personal presence of God to the knowledge and charity which arise from grace. It is only in these acts that the substantial reality of God becomes present to man as the very form and object of the dynamism of grace. God's dwelling in the souls of the just is thus a new and profound personal relationship, in which the trinitarian life of knowledge and love is shared in by man. By it, man's noblest activities are raised to the level of the tri-personal life of God. There is an actual contact, spiritual and mysterious but real, of man with the three divine persons.

PERSONAL COMMUNION   The divine persons dwell within the soul in their proper reality, so that even here on earth man is introduced into the life of personal communion with the Father, Son, and Spirit. St. Thomas sees this wonderful presence as a temporal extension of the eternal procession of the persons within the Trinity. Its effect is that the persons of the Trinity actually inhabit the soul of man. Indeed we may say that created grace is given in order that there may be a basis for the new presence of the Trinity within the Christian. This is not to say that any change occurs in God, but that in and through the created effects of grace and virtue man becomes newly present to the divine persons. 77 Grace and virtue constitute a living image of the Trinity within the soul. They enable the Christian, in his acts of knowledge and love, to realize within himself the unique presence of the Father, the Son, and the Holy Spirit. The divine persons thus assimilate the Christian through gifts of grace. The divine persons come to the Christian bestowing grace and the powers of grace. The very reality of these gifts unites man in a new way to Father, Son, and Spirit, enabling him to attain the living reality of the persons in his supernatural acts of living faith and charity.

Thus there are two aspects to the indwelling presence of the divine persons: the soul of the Christian is made like to the Father, Son, and Spirit in and through the gifts of grace. In this way there is realized a presence to the soul of the divine persons. Secondly, in the acts of faith and love, Father, Son, and Holy Spirit became real and present objects, even forms or formal objects of man's supernatural activity. *This means that the life of grace is seen above all as a life in personal communion and relationship with the triune God.* The created image of the Trinity given in the gifts of grace is made actual and living by those divine actions which constitute the reality of the friendship of God with man.

It is thus that Thomistic theology seeks to understand and express the new life of grace which has been described in the New Testament. This new life given in and through the redemptive work of Christ leads to new action by the Christian, who lives in him as a member of his body, the Church.

The New Law

Sanctifying grace is a new nature received in the soul in virtue of the divine causality. It is not a merely static gift but a new principle and source of action. Grace in its formal constitution is therefore a new efficiency or dynamism, the reality of which is manifest in human activity. Sanctifying grace touches the essence of the soul; with it come powers of new action in all aspects of man's life. Not only do these new powers act to give expression to the life of grace; they manifest that triumph over sin and the flesh and the Law which the New Testament portrays as fundamental to the being of the Christian. The Holy Spirit dwelling in the soul of the new man replaces the flesh, as it were, as a principle of action. The grace of the Spirit leads to a life of goodness as opposed to the former life of sin without grace. Indeed, in the thought of St. Thomas, the presence of the Holy Spirit is also liberation from

78

the Law, for the New Law *is* the dynamic presence of God in his gifts of grace.

LAW AND FREEDOM   The regime of Christ which replaces the regime of the Law is said by St. Thomas to be the dynamic reality of grace itself. "What is most fundamental in the law of the New Testament and what constitutes its whole power is the grace of the Holy Spirit given through faith in Christ. Basically, therefore, the reality of the grace of the Holy Spirit bestowed on the Christian is itself the New Law." (*S.Th.*, 1ª2ªᵉ, 106,1) The Christian is freed from a regime of the letter and is introduced into the new covenant which is principally the dynamic presence of grace. If grace itself is the basic meaning of the New Law, then we may see with St. Thomas that all other aspects of the life of the Christian are graces. Everything which contributes to and is needed for the life of the Christian is itself a grace. All relate, however, to what is basic and fundamental: the vital presence in grace of the divine persons.

The Christian is freed from the Law, but there are still laws within the Church. At times one may feel that the burden of the letter, the weight of laws and rules, is little different from that of the Old Law. On this point St. Thomas tells us: "Even the letter of the gospel would bring death, unless the inner and healing grace of faith were present." (*S.Th.*, 1ª2ªᵉ, 106,2) There is thus a great difference in the activity of man under the Old Law and in the living reality of the New. The legal prescriptions of the former covenant led to greater sin and death because the Law did not confer a new life and a new power of action. Moral rules were known, but without the power of the Spirit they could not be expressed in action as a new life. This is true of any code of rules or laws. It may direct to a life of virtue but it does not *give the power* of virtuous action.

The Holy Spirit

Quite different is the New Law which consists fundamentally and primarily in the regenerating presence of the Spirit. He bestows grace as a *power* of a new life. No longer are moral rules and the exhortations of the gospel merely rules of conduct. The letter of these laws is vivified in the power of the Spirit; for the Christian they now express the inner law, they are the natural expression of his new being. The activity of the Christian can never be a mere conformity to the dead letter of any law, even if the words of the law are written in the gospel. The Christian's actions are basically the concrete expression of his new life in Christ. They are the spontaneous manifestations of the operative power of the grace of the Spirit. As with any genuine life, grace seeks to manifest itself in action. Conversely, any such action is made possible by grace. The laws of the Christian life are nothing more or less than expressions of the way in which the power of grace is shown forth in action.

Not in any legalistic sense, then, will the Christian manifest his incorporation into Christ. He does it by activity made possible by the Spirit's dynamic presence.

Continuing Powers of Action: Infused Virtues

If the term *new nature* may be used of sanctifying grace, then *powers of action* may describe the abiding virtues of the supernatural life. Just as man's human nature expresses itself through such powers of action as the mind, the will, and the senses, so the new nature of grace expresses itself in new powers of action proportionate to the life of grace. (Cf. S.Th., 1ª2ae, 51;62–65) The being of man as a natural entity is manifested and developed only in the proper activities of man. Human action is at once the expression and perfection of the dynamic resources of his nature. So too is it in the order of grace, which as a new nature of man ("supernatural life") finds its dynamic perfection in activity which shows forth the power of the new life. If the Christian exists in the Spirit, he walks in the Spirit of newness by action which surpasses the capabilities of unredeemed and sinful man.

The actions of the Christian made possible by grace are not, of course, merely an active conformity to an arbitrary divine will. They are human acts that are in all respects proper to the divine will, free but not arbitrary; they express the reality of grace in a dynamic fashion. Sanctifying grace can be seen as necessary if man is to be made capable of attaining union with God in his own trinitarian life.

Since God wishes to give himself to man even in this life, in an anticipated possession of the realities of heaven, grace is bestowed. By it man is elevated to a sharing in the divine nature; he may possess the foundation of a new activity which itself is an anticipation of the activity of glory. Grace enters into man to such an extent that he is made capable of action which is at once the result of grace and of human 80 power. The divine causality of grace thus enhances and makes productive the causality of man. The reality of this is manifested in the fact that grace bestows continuing powers of new action. These are habitual graces, for they are given as *permanent* sources of action. They are also sometimes termed *operative*. Usually theology speaks of these new powers of action as the *infused virtues*—"infused" indicating their source in God, and "virtue" defining their character as abiding, operative principles (dynamic sources) of good action.

These graces are given to insure even further the activity of grace. By them man is united to God not only in his being but also in his action. The reality of these gifts is a proof of the insistence of Catholic theology on the inner reality of God's grace. Grace is a total organism of new life. It is neither exterior to man in the Protestant sense nor within man's unaided capacities (Pelagianism). The reality of God's gracious love is attested to by the reality of the gifts he bestows. To make the organism of grace a dynamic reality the infused virtues are given. They enable man to live the life of the Christian by an active and free cooperation with God.

THEOLOGICAL VIRTUES   Among the infused virtues an absolute primacy is to be accorded to faith, hope, and charity, the three *theological virtues*. It has been noted that the objective aspect of the divine indwelling means that by acts of knowledge and love man can attain to God in his proper reality. The Trinity is present to the soul as three individuals whom the Christian can know and love not only indirectly but directly in themselves. Man is made capable of actions which have God for their object. He is enabled to share in the knowledge and love which are proper to God alone. The Christian can come into contact with God by actions which are human actions performed by man, yet which are also divine actions, because they participate in what is uniquely divine. By his natural constitution man is totally incapable of an adequate knowledge or love which has God himself as its object. Activity which is essentially supernatural attains to God directly. It shares in the knowledge and love which only God can have. God knows and loves in his own personal and trinitarian life. No creature is capable of entering into this sphere of action by virtue of his own resources. But, as we have seen, God in his love has willed to elevate man to the plane of his own life. The foundation of man's elevation is sanctifying grace, but the *full expression* of man's entering in is realized in the possession and activity of the theological virtues. The human intellect and will are intrinsically elevated, that is, made capable of actions which are communications in the divine life itself. These virtues enable man to know and to love in a way totally beyond the capacities of his nature. They do this by attaining to God himself who is, in his personal reality and life, beyond the whole order of creation.

We are admitted into the inner life, the thoughts, and the love of a person only by that person's free giving of himself. From external observation we can never come to the inner depths of another person. So, too, man can never come to the inner and personal being of God from anything external to God himself. But God has chosen to enter into relations of personal friendship with man. To make this possible, the Christian is given the virtues of faith, hope, and charity as new and absolute capacities for new action.

All the Christian's good actions can be directed toward God as to their ultimate goal; by the power of intention all the acts of the Christian can give expression to his divine allegiance. Thus it is that the work and daily activity of the Christian can be directed to God and made expressive of union with him. The acts of the theological virtues, however, are on a different and higher plane still. These acts are not merely directed toward God. They attain to God himself in his proper reality. Thomistic theology expresses this truth in precise fashion by saying that any and all good actions of the Christian may have God as their term and goal, but only the theological virtues have God as their specific and proper object.

FAITH   Divine faith is the foundation of the Christian's new activity. In faith man is granted a share in that knowledge which God alone *is* and has. Faith is more than merely a knowledge about God; it is true knowledge of a kind proper to God himself. The act of faith is an assent to statements expressed in human words and concepts; assent to these words is a knowledge which comprises genuine mental contact with the realities expressed in the words. Assent is given to the statement that Christ is truly God and truly man, for example, but the knowledge of faith does not stop at the words. In and through the words faith comes to rest in a knowledge of the person of Christ. He is the reality the words express. By faith we know not only statements about Christ but Christ himself. In this we share in the divine knowledge, for it is only in God's knowledge of himself that we know the truth of Christ. The truth of the statements of faith are really the expressions of divine reality, since truth is the self-manifestation of being. In attaining to divine truth the act of faith attains to the divine being.

Through the formulations of Catholic belief the believer is united in mind to the divine realities manifested in its words and concepts. While this knowledge is not the vision of heaven, but a faith in what

82

is not seen, the reality of the knowledge of faith gives a grasp of divine being as it is in itself. The act of faith terminates in God, in the divine persons and their works. It thus produces contact with God in himself. The order of being is measured by the order of knowledge; the level of knowledge corresponds to that of reality. Faith is a divine knowledge of divine things.

A Unique Knowing. The unique knowledge that is faith is possible to us because it is rooted in God's manifestation of truths and realities. God speaks the words of faith to the mind of the believer. St. Thomas sees this divine speaking as the basis of the assent of faith. God, who is truth and knowledge—whose knowledge is himself—reveals to the believer the mysteries of his being and action. Revelation therefore is not only the historical fact of a divine communication to man, it is the ever-present, mysterious self-manifestation of God. The mystery of faith lies in God's communicating his own knowledge and thus his own reality, as truth, to man in and through the finite medium of human concepts. By faith man is assimilated in mind to divine reality; he shares in the knowing of God himself.

By providing mental contact with God and thus introducing the Christian into the world of divine being, faith remains the foundation of the life of the Christian. Knowledge gives the initial and basic grasp of reality. It is in the light of this knowledge that the Christian is enabled to direct his own life. *Faith gives the knowledge indispensable for the active seeking of God and his kingdom, for it introduces divine knowledge into human awareness.* Faith provides the foundation for all the value judgments of the Christian, since it gives a cognitive grasp of the whole meaning of reality and life. In the light of the knowing contact with God which faith alone can provide, the whole activity of the Christian is directed.

HOPE While the contact of the Christian with God is initiated and rooted in faith, it is completed in a "going out to God" in hope and charity. These two theological virtues are new capacities of the human will—divine capacities—by which the initial contact with God in faith is completed. A seeking of union with God, which is more than the mental union of knowledge, is the form taken by that sharing of the divine activity which we call the virtues of hope and charity.

The doctrine of hope, expressed particularly by St. Paul, is centered on the new order of life in Christ. The Christian, saved already in hope, presses on to the day of glory. He awaits the second coming when his share in Christ's resurrection will be completed. If faith gives contact with the reality of Christ's salvation and its completion in the resurrection, hope seeks the fulfillment of incorporation into Christ. While faith gives knowledge of this divine destiny, it also tells of the wholly transcendent character of the final state of the Christian. To this destiny man can come only by the power of Christ and the merciful exercise of the divine omnipotence. Theological hope attains to this loving power. It is thus a confidence in God and in Christ which is a sharing in the actual power by which God comprises the fullness of his own beatitude. The term and goal of hope is the glory of heaven, which is in turn participation in the resurrection of Christ.

Even on earth, however, there is an anticipated possession of this destiny, and this we call hope. Hope's object is not merely the subjective state of eternal happiness which the Christian desires. It is also and more truly God uniting man to himself in the person of the glorified Christ. Man can never enter into God and be wholly united to him by his own resources. Hope is therefore a reliance on the divine power, a contact with the loving and omnipotent God who wills to give himself to man. By theological hope the Christian who shares in God's power and relies on his love is directed to God and the Christ of glory. Theological hope does not rest on any personal good works, nor on any personal religious experience that supposedly gives assurance of salvation. By hope the Christian awaits the glorious Savior, in virtue of the power of God.

CHARITY   The new life of the Christian is founded in love. This love expresses the Father's nature—for "God is love"—manifested in Christ and exercised in the Spirit. The Christian is defined as one who loves God (cf. 1 Cor 2,9; Jas 1,12); his love which is theological charity is a participation in what is uniquely and properly divine, namely the love that God is. In human terms it may be said that the inner life of the Trinity is completed in the eternal procession of love which terminates in the Holy Spirit. It is in this love within the Trinity that charity participates. By charity the Christian shares in the personal and trinitarian expression of the divine goodness. If faith is a sharing in the knowing and the knowledge of God (in him the two are one), so charity is a sharing in the actual love of the divine persons.

84   In the Spirit and through Christ we love the Father. We do so with that same love which characterizes the divine life. Charity is a

sharing in that love by which God loves. It assimilates the Christian to the love of God which is God himself. By sharing the divine love, man is lifted above his normal capacity to love. He becomes capable of a love which has God himself, in the Trinity of persons, as its object. St. Paul tells us that this charity will remain always, even in heaven. (1 Cor 13,8) This indicates that the love of charity on this earth is the Christian's most perfect anticipation of the life of glory.

Again, as in all the theological virtues, charity attains to God by a sharing in what is proper to God alone—his love. On the basis of the contact with God through knowledge achieved in faith, charity tends beyond the order of knowledge to that union with God—real and personal—which is man's destiny. By charity the Christian can respond in love to that love of the Father which anticipates all the actions of the creature, and which is the basis of the whole order of salvation.

Love of Man.   In virtue of this sharing in love, the Christian is able to exercise the same love that Christ exercised for men. If charity is centered first upon God, it follows the expansion and extension of the love he bears his creatures, especially those who are fellow men to us. The love of others is not a love distinct from charity toward God. It is an expression to other men of that same divine love. We may conceive the divine love as originating in the Father, manifested in Christ, and communicated to man through the Spirit. This communication of divine love is, in turn, communicated by the Christian to his fellow man. Thus is the cycle of divine love completed. God's love, which the Christian shares in, is naturally and spontaneously expressive. The love that Christians bear to others is the manifestation of the love God shows them in Christ. Charity is the noblest and most perfect expression of the life of grace because it is rooted in union with God. The activity of faith and hope finds completion in charity. Charity will be the dynamic source and integrating motive of all truly Christian action.

The Infused Moral Virtues

Because the theological virtues enable the Christian to perform actions on a plane where he is totally helpless without grace, they constitute the essential, dynamic gifts of grace. They are the basis for the whole life of the Christian. This life is a life in the world and among men. If the Christian is capable of the transcendent acts of faith, hope, and charity, he is still to exercise his Christian being in the context of

By the very nature of the creature the same principles apply to the order of grace. In a sense, they apply with even greater force, because there is a greater reality to the creature's action in grace than in nature. The greater the reality of the creature's operation, however, the more apparent is his dependence on the God of grace. In considering the Thomistic understanding of actual grace it is important to keep in mind these principles of theological thought. One general principle of St. Thomas may be insisted upon: to derogate from the causality of the creature is to derogate from the causality of the Creator. He holds that if there is reality in the good and saving acts of the Christian, these realities depend on the God of grace: specifically on actual graces. If, too, the reality of the God of grace and the power of his love are maintained, then the reality of human action cannot be denied.

God and Human Action

The Thomistic theology of actual grace seeks to formulate a doctrine which will lead to a clearer understanding of the dependence of the free, saving, human act on divine grace. This act will be at once *wholly* the effect of God and of his grace, and (because of this) *wholly* and truly human, affecting genuine human powers of action. In the order of grace man is dependent on God not only for his new being in Christ but also for his Christian activity, itself a form of being. Activity, because it is being, is as dependent on grace as any other form of being in the order of salvation. Apart from divine creativity the state of grace is a new possibility. Its activities are but "the possibilities of a possibility, the shadows of a shadow." (A.-D. Sertillanges, *Saint Thomas d'Aquin* [Paris, F. Alcan, 1925], I, 234) Under the divine creativity what is merely possible—as state and as actions—becomes actual. The Thomistic teaching on actual grace is exemplary of this basic truth. There is no confusion of the divine and the human, thus no hint of seeing God (or grace) and man (or his freedom) on the same plane of action. God and man (or grace and freedom) are not in competition as *coordinated* causes. They are on different levels of being and action, as transcendent principle and subordinate principle. God's grace is not then destructive of the reality of man's action but is *creative* of that action.

The Necessity of Actual Grace

Supernatural acts, to be such, demand the work of grace. By it, man is moved to will and to perform salutary actions. Supernatural grace is required for what the creature does beyond the capacities of his being, which means that actual operation is the result of the supernatural powers of action bestowed on man. The actions themselves are new actualities. They are activities, and not the power to engage in the activities. The new reality of supernatural action is dependent on the creative act of grace. This is given precisely as creative of the will to the new action (the new being) and its performance. While St. Thomas treats of this whole question in detail (*S.Th.*, 1ª2ᵃᵉ, 109), it will suffice for the present to note the following points.

Both in the order of knowledge and in the moral order of action, actual grace is absolutely and physically necessary for both assent to divine truth and the performance of any deed which is effectively supernatural. This necessity is said to be absolute and physical, rather than merely relative and moral, because man without grace is simply incapable of any action which pertains to the order of salvation. The assistance of grace, including the grace of revelation, may be morally necessary for acquiring other knowledge and performing naturally good works. It is *absolutely required* for actions which are truly supernatural.

We have seen that the whole process of coming to the faith, of embracing it, and of being justified demands the assistance of grace. This dependency of man, even justified and sanctified man, on grace is an abiding condition inherent in the nature of the creature. If man's action is supernatural it depends on supernatural grace. A correct religious and metaphysical understanding of the relation of man to God involves the truth that in every realization of being or action in the order of salvation, man is dependent on the grace of God. The gospel phrase that "without me you can do nothing" may be taken as a basic principle in the theology of actual grace.

This grace is distinct both from the uncreated action of God himself and from the human acts which depend on grace. *Rather it is a qualitative motion of the soul which is not habitual but transitory in nature. It is ordained to specific human acts and not to permanent principles of action.* In virtue of this created actual grace man is moved to supernatural action and to cooperation with the power of grace thus bestowed.

Sufficient and Efficacious Actual Grace

The best known distinction with regard to actual grace is that between sufficient and efficacious grace. A detailed explanation of this

distinction would go beyond present purposes. It would involve the repe-
tition of a great deal of controversial material expressing the views of the
Thomist and Molinist theologians. We shall restrict ourselves to several
basic points made by the Thomistic school in the light of general positions mentioned above. We shall maintain that the teaching of "Thomistic" theologians on this controverted point is in accord with the general theological position of St. Thomas. Thomas has a sound understanding of the relation of supernatural action to divine grace. All
Catholics admit the existence of these two forms of actual grace as resulting from the Church's definitions against heretical positions. These
points of essential agreement will be considered before stating the
Thomistic explanation of the nature of and difference between these
forms of divine assistance.

There is a grace given which is *truly sufficient* for the real and
actual possibility of supernatural action. This grace is truly and really
sufficient in its own order: that of conferring, in a transitory way, the
actual capacity for a good and saving act. To say this is to deny, as Catholic teaching does deny, the Jansenist view that all grace is fully irresistible. It is thus false to say that no true internal grace is given to
the person who seems to resist the impulse of grace. This grace is truly
sufficient in itself and in its own order of real possibility; it is also termed
merely sufficient, for this grace is resisted by man's free fault and refusal.
The actual good act is therefore never done.

There is also *efficacious* grace, which causes the good act and is
called efficacious precisely because its effect is seen in the good action.
Not only is the possibility to do God's will bestowed by God (sufficient
grace), but also the capability of the good and meritorious act is equally
God's work. The will to perform the good act and the actual doing of it
depend equally on efficacious grace. As we have seen (Chapter II), the
whole work of man's salvation is the gift of God and his loving grace.
Grace does not merely give the possibility to act well. It begets the good
act itself. In this sense the basic intuitions of St. Augustine gave expression to this divine truth.

The need for efficacious grace is such that without it man is incapable of salutary acts. It is commonly held to be theologically certain
that there is an infallible connection between the bestowal of efficacious
grace and the actual doing of the supernatural action.

Theological Differences

The precise nature of these forms of grace and the difference between them is matter for theological discussion. The problem centers around the meaning of that infallible connection between efficacious grace and the good action. The efficacy of grace must be upheld—just as the liberty of man under, in, and through this grace, must be. It has already been seen that the teaching of the Church involves both the efficacy of grace and the freedom of man.

Briefly the Molinists see sufficient grace made efficacious by the free consent of the will alone. Others hold that such grace is intrinsically efficacious, that is, of its very nature. Some explain this internal efficacy by an indifferent divine premotion. The latter is related to the actual being and not to the specific determination of the good act. Thomistic theologians explain the nature of efficacious grace by holding that the internal efficacy of this grace is the result of a so-called *predetermining, physical premotion* of God. In spite of the wording, this phrase has no reference to *time* as such, but to the transcendent divine causality which anticipates the good deed. The divine causality is said to be physical. It is called a motion to indicate the actual reality of the effect of divine action. But this action is not a physical motion in any ordinary sense of these words. It is not in any way on the *same level* of causality as man's but on the ontologically different, divinely transcendent plane. God's action is not a motion like man's but a creative act which is uniquely divine.

A Thomistic View

This is a determinate or "determining" action, because it is specific and even unique. It is a motion leading to this particular good act—not indifferently or generally to good acts. Thus the particular free choice of the Christian, the being and reality of his act, are understood to be *wholly the product of grace.* His choice is also *wholly the free act of a man.* His free human activity is divine activity even though he acts as a creature and not with the transcendent creative freedom of God. In and through the divine causality both man's freedom and his particular free act are dependent for their being on the divine motion. It is only when freedom is seen, in one way or another, as an emancipation from God that this doctrine appears contrary to liberty. A correct understanding of the reality of human freedom under grace sees it as dependent on the divine causality exercised in creative love. The ultimate goal of this love is to unite man to the life of God through activities which are truly human and free.

TWO EFFECTS OF GRACE

Justification

The essential points of the Catholic teaching on justification have been seen in the consideration of St. Paul's doctrine and that of the Council of Trent. Justification is understood as that effect of grace by which man is transformed from sin and the power of sin into new life in Christ. As a process over the course of time, justification is the leading of man from sin to life, from aversion from God to friendship. The moment of justification is that instant in which the actual infusion of sanctifying grace is realized: it is the moment of transformation involving the liberation from sin and death and the transfer of man interiorly into the life and kingdom of Christ. Man is prepared for this decisive moment of grace by the aid of many actual graces. This divine assistance is universally required for all actions which lead effectively to justification. This is true whether one is speaking of *first* justification (the initial conversion to God) or *second* justification (by which the Christian who has lost grace by sin comes back into the fellowship of the Holy Spirit). God's grace leads man to the moment of transformation by awakening both sorrow for sin and a knowledge and desire for salvation.

The acts which lead to justification include those of the mind and of the will. In first justification the essential knowledge to be gained is that of faith, so that man is led to supernatural knowledge by internal and external graces. This knowledge of salvation leads to an awareness of sin as a moral reality which prevents man's own salvation, and which ultimately is known in its full reality as an offense against God. Positively, this new knowledge awakens the active hope of salvation in Christ and some form of love for God, the author and giver of salvation. In all these acts God works with loving care to lead this particular person to himself. These acts, which include at least the implicit desire for baptism, reach their highest moment in the instant of justification itself.

THE CAUSE OF JUSTIFICATION   Objectively the cause of justification is the redeeming work of Christ communicated at the moment of the bestowal of sanctifying grace. This involves not only the infusion of new life but the destruction of sin. These are not two distinct acts of God. The very incorporation into Christ involves the forgiveness of sin and the real destruction of the inner forces of evil. God does not unite man to himself without simultaneously destroying sin and the power of

92

sin, both of which separate man from God. In this act of justification the sacraments of baptism and penance are instrumental causes of the communication of divine love and pardon. The work of justification is a divine action uniting man to God and bestowing on him a new principle of life which by its nature excludes sin and evil.

MAN'S COOPERATION   Justification, however, is not a work which God accomplishes in us without our free cooperation. There are free acts on our part which are the essential concomitants of the bestowal of grace. This does not mean in any sense that these acts are good works which earn justification for man. St. Paul and Catholic tradition see these acts as essential elements of justification which really and causally depend on grace, and which are the subjective causes of justification. The act of living faith, informed by charity and accompanied by sorrow for sin, is the moment of man's cooperation with the new life. In this sense living faith is the conscious act of man's freedom which is at once the ultimate internal disposition for grace and the concomitant of the coming of sanctifying grace. This act of faith is itself the result of both grace and the essential cooperation of man with the infusion of grace. In this act man freely opens himself to Christ and his redeeming act by a faith which assents to the meaning of salvation. His assent is informed by a love or charity which embraces Christ the Redeemer.

The moment of justification is the real beginning of glory in heaven, for it has its existence with reference to the ultimate union with God to be accomplished in glory. In this life, justification is the basis for the whole activity of the Christian. It is the communication of a divine life which is to grow and increase in intensity by the activity whch is the manifestation of a new being. Grace is given at justification in varying degrees, according to the measure of God's will and the essential dispositions of man. The grace given is to be expressed in good works by further cooperation with grace, so that this new life will become a progressive assimilation to Christ.

Merit

It is in the doctrine of merit that we see how continual cooperation with grace intensifies the life of union with Christ, both in this life and in the triumph of glory. The essentials of Catholic dogma on merit have been seen above, with emphasis on the following points. God wishes to communicate himself to man in the life of grace, to such an extent that man can actually cooperate with God's gifts. The dogma of merit ex-

93

presses the full reality of human cooperation by emphasizing the inevitable result of the structure of good action performed under grace and charity. Merit comes only with those free acts which are fully good, in that they depend on the state of grace and are informed by the ultimate power of divine charity. The bond of charity linking man with Christ enables man to merit for his own works. This is in no sense a merit opposed to or in competition with the total merit of Christ. While many Protestants see the doctrine on merit as derogatory to the plenitude of Christ's meritorious redemption, the Catholic sees human merit as fully dependent on the merits of Christ. Indeed the reality of our merit is but an expression of the reality of the communication of Christ's saving merits. United to Christ, the true life (Jn 15,5) by grace and charity, the Christian is made capable of meritorious free acts which express the vitality of union with Christ.

TYPES OF MERIT   Merit concretely is the good act in its quality of relation to a reward or recompense. In the present order of salvation, and in dependence on the merits of Christ, theologians distinguish two forms of supernatural merit. *Condign* merit rests upon the divinely established just order by which recompense is given as something truly earned. In this sense condign merit results from the inner order of divine justice, in which a proportionate reward is given to man's actions. Analogous to this is *congruous* or congruent merit, in which the reward is given not in the divine justice but precisely from the loving mercy of God who bestows congruent merit as a fitting expression of his friendship with man.

Actually, of course, the whole order of merit is the order of divine love and mercy. Within this order, however, theologians legitimately distinguish these two forms of merit by reason of the inner connection, in justice or simply in mercy, of the good act with its supernatural reward. (Cf. S.*Th.*, 1ª2ᵃᵉ, 21,3 and 4;114.)

CONDITIONS OF MERIT   Since merit rests on the state of grace and the presence of charity, there is no meritorious action before justification; the first step which man takes toward justification is totally gratuitous and *un*merited. Furthermore the various acts which man performs through grace, and which lead to justification, do not merit justification unless one uses merit in a very loose and metaphorical sense. It is only in the activity of the justified Christian that merit is found in its true meaning. Seeking to make more precise the statements of the

94

Council of Trent, theologians give further expression to the general doctrine of meriting an increase of grace and eternal life.

Thus the Christian can gain an increase in the intensity and degree of sanctifying grace and the infused virtues by condign merit. By his good, free acts performed under the influence of charity in the state of grace the Christian can earn the crowning reward of eternal life with condign merit. However, man cannot earn the condign merit of recovering the state of grace after a mortal sin. Mortal sin destroys the whole basis of merit. The sinner may expect God's loving grace, but he cannot strictly merit the recovery of a gift he has freely rejected. In general man may merit those things necessary for his Christian life. This includes, says St. Thomas, even those material and temporal goods which may be necessary for eternal life. In sum, man may merit both condignly and congruously for himself in the order of grace.

Man can merit only congruently for others; this is possible in virtue of the bond of charity and the unity of all men in Christ. St. Thomas would even hold that man can merit the grace of justification for others with truly congruous if not condign merit. In this way the Christian may actively cooperate in the divine work of salvation by his prayers and good works, which can lead even to the conversion and new life of others. The Christian is invited, therefore, to action in behalf of his fellows. Prayer is the first thing the Christian does for others but he also may work for them, for the good of the whole Church and of all mankind, by the meritorious power of his actions.

MERIT AND DEATH   The final triumph of the Christian is his death in Christ. We have seen the reality of the conquering of death in speaking of New Testament teaching. It may now be asked whether the Christian truly merits what theologians call the gift of final perseverance. This gift is precisely death in Christ, the actual coincidence of the moment of death with the life or state of grace. The gift of perseverance remains a gift and is not, properly speaking, the object of merit. The reason for this is that this state of grace is not itself the object but rather the source and principle of merit. Man cannot merit that which is the source of merit, but the state of grace continued to the end of life or joined with the moment of death is the source of merit. The gift of final perseverance is an object of hope and prayer, and God does not abandon those who do not first abandon him. At the end of the *Our Father* we pray for this final deliverance from evil. In the *Hail Mary* the Christian asks the aid of the Mother of God at the hour of death.

Man merits life eternal, the goal of the life of grace and its activities in this life. Meriting eternal life is an aspect of all the good works of grace performed by free man. But final perseverance is not eternal life. It is rather the reality of the state of grace in this life, and indeed at the supreme moment of this life. Thus the object of this gift of perseverance is the source of merit, not its effect.

A New Life

In its structure and meaning, the gift of grace is a new life given as a permanent and abiding reality. Man may freely reject this gift, but in itself it is the seed of glory and in its activities it brings an anticipation of the very life of the Trinity. The death of the Christian is the final liberation from sin, the flesh, and sinful death. It is thus the entrance into the fullness of that life of grace which is the anticipated possession of the life of glory. In this life the Christian is saved in hope. In the life of glory the life of grace remains—transformed by the vision of the divine persons, whose presence was already realized in some measure in the life of grace.

NOTE ON BAIUS
AND JANSENIUS

During the Council of Trent and in the years following it, Catholic theologians sought a renewed understanding of the theology of grace. Because of the prominence of the notion of predestination in Reformation thought—particularly in Calvinism—a great deal of discussion centered on the explanation of the relationship between divine predestination and human freedom. While the discussion is not within the limits of this volume, we may say that these theological investigations sought a more complete and correct understanding of grace and predestination, their mutual interrelation, and their effect on human causality and free action. Both groups of disputants sought a more precise formulation of the double and simultaneous realities of divine and human agency in the work of salvation, and eventually in the whole area of man's dependence on God in being and action. For our present purposes we shall mention only certain limited aspects of two closely related heretical systems developed by theologians who sought an explanation of predestination and grace through an uncomplicated return (as they conceived it) to the thought of St. Augustine. Our concern is only with the notions of grace advanced in these systems, not with the whole question of divine knowledge and predestination.

BAIUS

The theories of Baius (Michel de Bay, c.1513–1589) are not especially profound and represent a peculiar, even paradoxical union of elements of both   *97* Pelagian and Protestant thought. Since the examination of the supernatural state of Adam is treated elsewhere in this series, it is sufficient to state here that Baius conceived of it as identified with the constitution of man's nature. The following opinion of Baius was among the list of his views condemned by Pope St. Pius V in 1567: "The exalting of human nature to a participation of the divine nature was due to the integrity of man in his first state, and for that reason should be called natural, not supernatural." (D1021; TCT608; cf. D1055,1078; TCT609f.) This assertion confuses the natural and the supernatural, or more accurately put, reduces the supernatural to the level of the natural. If grace is bestowed as part of the "integrity of nature" or of man, then it will be neither gratuitous nor, of course, genuine grace. An essential notion of grace—that it be seen and received by man as a free gift of a loving God—is hence denied. The source of Baius' error seems to lie in his too extrinsecist and superficial view of grace, which overlooks the inner reality of this elevating and sanctifying relationship with God.

The Result of Sin

As a result of original sin, Baius continues, man's state is radically changed. The Walloon thinker seems to envisage the results of the fall in a Lutheran perspective. Specifically, man's freedom is seen as totally corrupt, so that, "Without the help of God's grace, free will can do nothing but sin." (D1077; TCT619; cf. D1025,1028; TCT618,620.) Fallen man is the complete victim of disordered desires, in this view. Baius has not only failed to appreciate the intrinsically gratuitous and supernatural character of grace; he has failed to appreciate the reality and self-consistency of nature. Nature and freedom, consequently, seem completely destroyed by the fall.

The whole life and activity of the non-Christian are conceived of by Baius as sinful. Not only is he incapable of any good action. He actually sins in all his activity. (D1038–1040) In this view of the depravity of fallen man, Baius shares the outlook of Reformation theology. His opinions were condemned as contrary to the orthodox understanding of Catholic tradition.

Baius is erroneous both with respect to the doctrine of the truly supernatural state to which Adam was elevated and the understanding of man's nature after the fall. Behind these extreme views lies the double failure of a misconception of the orders of grace and nature. If the gifts of grace are part of the original constitution and essential structure of man's being, then the loss of these gifts, in the mind of Baius, entails the practical destruction of freedom and the complete servitude of man to sin.

Grace and Justification

In the light of these positions, it is not difficult to realize that Baius has
98 misinterpreted the nature of grace and justification. From one point of view, his system makes no allowance for a proper theological notion of sanctifying

grace—partly because Baius has a superficial, moralistic view of the relationship of God and man. Yet he wishes to retain the defined dogmas of Trent.
How are these to be understood? Because he lacked any sound metaphysical or
theological foundation, it is inevitable that Baius should have interpreted the
doctrine of grace in an extrinsecist sense. While in reality he comes close to a
Lutheran, external view of justification as mere imputation, he does not express his ideas in Lutheran terminology. It may be said that his doctrine on
justification is a sort of unhappy compromise which is neither fully Lutheran
nor fully Augustinian, or Catholic.

Ignoring the inner transformation of man in sanctifying grace, Baius
conceives of justification as the restoring of man's power to act well. It is not,
however, a power to do good rooted in a genuine renewal of man. It appears
to be justified man's imperfect imitation of true justice. He is liberated from
sin, but Baius then seems to subject man's freedom to a necessitating grace. It
seems that the state of justice is conceived merely as a succession of acts, some
good, some evil. The evil acts are owing to man's remaining sinfulness, while
the good acts are attributed to a power of grace which appears to operate without any genuine human cooperation. Distinguished from Luther by this insistence on the good works of the justified man, the thought of Baius cannot
seem to conceive a real, inner principle of good action bestowed by grace. He
is content to describe the state of grace in terms of a moralism centered on
good deeds performed by grace. The following summary statement of Baius'
thought was formally condemned:

> The justice by which the sinner is justified through faith consists
> formally in the observance of the commandments, which is the justice
> of works. It does not consist in a [habitual] grace infused into the
> soul, by which man is adopted into divine sonship and is interiorly
> renewed and made a sharer in the divine nature, so that renewed
> through the Spirit by this grace, he is enabled to live a holy life and
> obey the divine commands. (D1042)

Baius denies a genuine renovation of man, that is, that justified man receives
a real inner principle of good action. He limits the notion of justification and
grace to an external observance of law and obedience to the commandments.
In reality Baius' notion of grace is only an unstable imitation of grace.

God and Man

Here again, it may be noted, the central problem is a faulty understanding of the nature of the relationship between God and man. God's action in
grace is seen as so external and anthropomorphic that the relations between God and man are reduced to those of a supreme and just master and
a weak and disobedient servant. The latter hardly possesses any real
capacity for action. As for the action of God in justification and in the justified man, Baius seems to conceive of the divine causality in an occasionalistic

setting. That is to say, without God's causing in man a real, inner principle of good action, God acts occasionally—in an off and on manner—in order to effect good deeds. God does not act on the justified man, in Baius's system, in any real and stable sense. He bestows on occasion a necessitating grace which produces the good deed. One of the condemned statements reads, for example: "In the Scriptures, freedom does not mean freedom from necessity but only freedom from sin." (D1041; *TCT*622) This statement reveals a notion of freedom which is merely external and purely verbal. What takes place, it seems, according to Baius, is an occasional substitution of God's necessary action for man's in the state of justification. This position obviously departs from the sound notion of human freedom and causality upheld by the Council of Trent. It is likewise derogatory to the divine causality, which is really lessened if conceived of as a mere anthropomorphic substitute for human action. This central error in Baius lies behind the particular aberrations noted above.

Summary

In conclusion, it is well to recall that the condemnation of Baius provided the Church the occasion for the proper interpretation of the decrees of Trent. It was an opportunity to state clearly that the gift of grace is truly supernatural: that is, that grace is always a free gift of God's love, in no way demanded for the integral constitution and inner consistency of human nature. By the free and merciful love of God man is destined to a life of intimate personal union with God in this life and in the next. Man can never respond to this gift unless it is recognized for what it truly is: a gift which surpasses all purely human or created reality. Thus, again, the statement of doctrine is not merely a matter of external orthodoxy, but a necessary intellectual condition of the religious relationship of man to God in Christ.

JANSENISM

Historically, Jansenism is more than a system of thought. Developing into a sect, it became responsible for a whole religious and spiritual mentality. It exerted a far from beneficial influence on religious behavior and outlook. Our concern is not with this movement *in toto* but with the teaching on grace developed by Cornelius Jansen (Jansenius, 1585–1638). As with Baius, on whom he depended in many ways, Jansen sought to arrive at a pure theology of grace by a return to the study of Augustine. His great work, the celebrated *Augustinus*, was published in 1640 after his death. It shortly became the center of much controversy. From this work various statements were gleaned which were made the object of formal condemnation by Pope Innocent X in 1653. Jansen accepted in large measure the false reading of Augustine found in Baius. He tended to see an excessive opposition between the condition of human nature in Adam before the fall and the state of human nature in fallen man. As with Baius the original situation of Adam was viewed in what may be called Pelagian perspectives. Part of the human endowment was a wholly self-sufficient freedom. Created "grace" was seen as part of the reality of man to such an extent that salvation would be no more than a spontaneous expression of liberty. The state of fallen man, however, was understood in excessively pessimistic terms. It is with Jansen's understanding of grace in the present state of religious reality that we are directly concerned.

Sin and Human Damnation

The whole of fallen humanity is logically destined to eternal damnation: the infidel world of nonbelievers, deprived of grace and representing the majority of mankind, moves toward perdition. This is a just view for Jansen, because grace to be gratuitous cannot be offered to all men. Therefore salvation is for the few to whom God gives faith and grace. Such is Jansen's highly deterministic understanding of predestination. What of the believers? Jansen actually denies grace to the believer. It is indeed only to those absolutely predestined that God gives an invincible grace which assures their salvation. Eventually this idea will develop, among Jansen's followers, into a notion of salvation; saved are the élite among the faithful who are possessed by grace and are moved inexorably, through a somber and unique spirituality, to heaven. This fundamentally pessimistic outlook on man and the limitation of God's grace is central to Jansenist mentality in its later stages of development. In regard to Jansen himself, the Church condemns as false this statement: "It is semi-Pelagian to say that Christ died or shed his blood for all men without exception." (D1096; *TCT*631) The proposition is declared to be not only false but heretical in the strict sense, if it is interpreted to mean that Christ died only for the predestined. Thus the Church condemned Jansen's key notion, in which he expressed an excessive predestinationism and a pessimism derogatory to the reality of God's universal will to salvation.

Predestination

The rigid predestinationism of Jansen, coupled with an excessively narrow reading of St. Augustine, forms the basis of the Jansenist understanding of freedom and grace. To this may be added the fact that Jansen intentionally passed over the great medieval theology on grace. Like Baius, he failed to consider the theological reality of man's divinization by the gift of sanctifying grace. How then did he conceive the justification of fallen man? First of all, man's freedom was seen as incapable of any good (even natural good) without grace. Deprived of grace, man sins by a natural spontaneity. In other words fallen man is inexorably drawn to damnation. Later the philosopher Pascal would express this Jansenist (and ultimately Protestant) outlook on man in such dramatic descriptions as man the chaos, man the chimera, the "feeble earthworm," the "man of uncertainty," the "pride and refuse of the universe." (*Pensées*, 434) It is original sin which is the main key to man's state (*Ibid.*, 441); wretched man yearns for escape from the despair, sinfulness and misery of this chaotic condition.

It is a basically Protestant understanding of fallen man which lies behind the Jansenist consideration of the need of salvation. Fallen man is beyond redemption, or at least beyond a redemption which would transform him from within. This, of course, is not the Catholic notion of fallen man, in which man retains the essential consistency in his nature. The Catholic sees him as capable of renovation and healing. Jansenism tends to take a Calvinistic view of man before God, in which, by virtue of an absolute predestination, the weak, fragile, and corrupt being of sinful man is seized by God's grace and made the instrument of the divine will; yet all this transpires without an inner reformation, so that fallen man remains fallen. He remains incapable of the good as well as of the gift of grace understood in a Catholic sense.

The Notion of Grace

How exactly does Jansenism conceive of grace? Within its framework, there is the fundamental Protestant yearning of the individual for absolute assurance of salvation. In Pascal's terms: for man "our true and only virtue is to hate ourselves and to seek a truly lovable Being to love." (*Pensées*, 468) How does man come to this? In "God *experienced* by the heart." In other words, the distinctively Protestant and individualistic view of salvation leads to seeing the sole hope for fallen man in a triumphant seizing of man by God in grace, whereby assurance of salvation is attained. This is far different from the Augustinian thought: "Hope not in yourself, but in your God"; "Even when confessing his sins, man should confess them with the praise of God." (*Discourses on the Psalms* 41,12; 105,2)

Augustine's real awareness of man's fallen state led to hope in God and his grace, to man's self-surrender to God, but not to a forcing of God into the confines of man's subjective experience. Despite his profound awareness of grace St. Augustine never sought to possess God in this Protestant or Jansenist sense. God comes as a person comes, to be adored and loved, not as the personal possession and assurance of man. In the depths of the Augustinian experience of God is a profound reverence and a great hope, but never a bringing down of God to where he becomes subject and subjected to the experience of the creature. It is quite different for the Jansenist. Pascal will cling to the paradoxical experience of fallen man's having God in his heart while he remains a chaos.

Grace then comes irresistibly to fallen man for Jansen. One of his most distinctive heretical doctrines is his teaching on irresistible grace, on the overwhelming, victorious movement of the will called *"delectatio victrix"*—the conquering pleasure or joy which is efficacious grace—the only grace of any consequence. Given man's fallen condition, God acts on man by causing an irresistible attraction to what is good, a pleasure so powerful that man always yields to this power. Man then is not truly free in the Catholic sense. Jansen demands only an external freedom from external necessity.

Merit

That is surely why the following statement was condemned: "To merit or demerit in the state of fallen nature it is not necessary for a man to have freedom from necessity but only freedom from constraint." (D1094; *TCT*629) According to Jansen man's freedom is passive before the onslaught of grace. This grace is never resisted; it is always efficacious. The Church likewise condemned this Jansenist declaration: "In the state of fallen nature internal grace is never resisted." (D1093; *TCT*628) The following proposition was condemned by the Church because it gives a false interpretation of semi-Pelagianism and clearly implies the Jansenist notion of irresistible grace. "The Semipelagians admitted the necessity of internal, preparatory grace for individual acts, even for the beginning of faith [this is Jansen's false interpretation of what to him was the Church's wrong condemnation of these earlier heretics]; they were heretics for this reason, that they admitted this grace to be such that the human will could either resist it or obey it." (D1095; *TCT*630)

Irresistible Grace

Jansen explained the fall of just men or believers by a lack of irresistible grace. To him, some commandments seemed impossible. The Church upheld the contrary, maintaining that grace is given to the just to observe the commandments of God, which is to say that for the justified man obedience to the essential law of God is possible through grace. But man, in Catholic teaching, can resist grace and thus fall into sin. That meant that another aspect of Jansen's teaching was condemned as heretical: "There are some of God's commandments that just men cannot observe with the power they have in their present state, even if they wish and strive to observe them; nor do men have the grace which would make their observance possible." (D1092; *TCT*627)

The notion of irresistible grace, Jansen claimed, came from his reading of St. Augustine. Augustine, it is true, described the action of the free will of man—the power of free choice or *liberum arbitrium*—as a love or joy centering on the various objects of freedom. In fact, liberty was this inner movement to certain objects of choice. True goodness becomes the object of love and joy for the Christian as a result of grace. *In a truly Pauline sense, grace gives man his true liberty.* Grace inspires in man a love of the good and a delight in God impossible to sinful man. "'I delight in the law of God according to the inner man'; but this delight in the good, by which man, out of a love of justice and not merely out of a fear of punishment, does not consent to evil, is to be attributed only to grace." (St. Augustine, *Against Two Letters of Pelagius*, I, 10,22PL)

Jansen and Augustine

Augustine sees grace as freeing man from bondage to sin and giving to the power of free choice the capacity to love justice and seek God. Indeed this is true liberty, the liberty of the children of God; and this ability to take delight in and to pursue the good is the work of God's grace in us. As Gilson notes, however (*The Christian Philosophy of St. Augustine* [New York: Random House, 1960], p. 322, n. 81) Jansen separated two things seen as a unity by Augustine. For Augustine, the delight in justice was itself the love of the will freed by grace; the power of free choice itself was liberated and made capable of this love which was its own act. By the power of grace man could in his own will take active delight in God and his holy law. But Jansen did not have this penetrating vision into the radical reformation of man's powers. Therefore he conceived of delight or pleasure as a force quite heterogeneous to and different from the will itself. As an external force it caused the will to act in a certain way. Jansen thought of the delight caused by grace as something from the outside caused by God, irresistibly moving man to act in a definite way and thus destroying man's freedom. Far from being an authentic Augustinian, Jansen had read into St. Augustine his own personal thoughts. Jansen thus misconceives the whole nature of God's operation within man. He fails to appreciate the reality of sanctifying grace, and he sees irresistible grace as a divine substitute for genuine human action. In Pascal's terms, the paradox of sinful man is resolved by making man the mere instrument of an overwhelming divine action. God is "experienced in the heart," but at the cost of a true Catholic understanding of the nature of grace and of the creative love of God for man.

Conclusion

As noted above, Jansenism became a strong sect, adhering to its doctrines and spiritual outlook in face of the opposition of the Church. The rigid, somber, almost Calvinistic mentality of Jansenism had great and lasting influence in religious life and thought. On several occasions the Church officially intervened to denounce erroneous or heretical views that were being perpetuated. One such instance was the official condemnation in 1713 of a series of false doctrines proposed by Pasquier Quesnel who had become the spiritual leader and guide of Port-Royal, near Paris (center of Jansenist piety and thought). Quesnel maintained a general position which was a synthesis of the views of Baius and Jansenius: a restatement of all their errors compounded and amplified. He boldly proclaimed his adherence to the Jansenist view of irresistible grace. One of the condemned propositions shows this latter point clearly: "Grace is nothing more than God's omnipotent will commanding and doing what he commands." (D1361; *TCT*642; cf. *TCT*632,644.) This statement of the heretical understanding of grace is an astute affirmation of the whole principle of God's sole agency in the order of salvation. By it inner, created grace is denied and man himself has no agency in the order of grace.

The vigorous reaction of the Church against these errors provides a clear indication of the significance of a sound and orthodox understanding of the Catholic teaching on this mystery.

GLOSSARY

acquired virtue: see *virtue.*

adoptive sonship: see *sonship.*

analogous—analogy of being: this notion arises from reflection on the real similarity of things as well as on their dissimilarity. A man may be good, a house may be good, a car may be good: all are good but in different ways. The concept of goodness is said to be *analogous* with respect to its various realizations. There is a real analogy between God and his creatures. God is intelligent and man is intelligent but each in a different way. Whereas God is intelligence by his very nature, man possesses intelligence as a result of divine causality and creation. This real similarity means that man can know about God and speak of him in words which have reference to creatures. In the order of revelation, we speak of the "analogy of faith." This means that the words and terms of divine revelation have meaning for man because he can discover their significance. Thus, God is called Father, and the Second Person is called the Son. These are not meaningless statements because the words Father and Son have a real meaning for man even though their immediate human meaning must be immeasurably extended to refer to what is properly divine. Grace is said to be an analogous participation by man in the nature of God. This means that what is proper and unique to God is shared in by man in some similar, analogous way.

communion: a union with or a participation in something along with others. Man has communion with other men by possessing common humanity with them. Man has communion with God by sharing in divine life. In a more active sense, men can be in communion by sharing in a common activity. In the order of salvation, God and man can be in communion, e.g., by sharing in love.

dynamic: having to do with the order of action and the exercise of power, as contrasted with the more "static" view of a thing. To illustrate, anatomy studies structures of the body, e.g., the arrangement of the skeletal or muscle structure, whereas physiology studies the action of man and his physical structures. The consideration of anatomy is *static*, that of physiology is *dynamic*. In theology, grace can be considered statically as a likeness or similarity to God, but it may also be considered dynamically as a power giving rise to new actions.

"extrinsecist": in the context of the theology of grace, this is a view of God's action which does not see that God really acts within man; his action remains outside of or "extrinsic" to him. Nothing happens within man, he is not actually changed, in this view of his justification. God merely considers man justified without acting in him. Catholic theology would hold that in justification God enters into man and changes him from within by communicating the new life of grace.

function: the function of something is its activity, the action proper to it. Thus, the function of the mind is to think so as to interpret experience; the function of an automobile is to provide transportation. In the order of revelation, Christ exercises a function, an activity, proper to him as man's savior and redeemer. The functions or activities of grace in man are the expressions in action of a new life given to him by Christ. Faith, hope, and charity can be called functions or activities of the state of grace.

grace: (a) theology speaks of *Uncreated Grace,* meaning God himself in his relation to man—sanctifying him, joining man to himself, and communicating himself to man. In relating himself to man in this way God is acting out of his free love, i.e., graciously, gratuitously, and without compulsion. Because of this gracious character of God's relation to man, God himself is called gracious or is said to be himself Uncreated Grace. (b) *created grace:* the reality produced in man by God's creative love; this reality is not God himself, but is the result of God's action within man. It is called a grace because it is the result of the gracious love of God, and is received by man as a favor or free gift. It can be either a *permanent reality* inhering within him as something real and constant, or a *transient reality* enabling man to perform actions in the order of salvation. The former is called *habitual grace* (the Latin word "habitus" refers to an enduring quality and not just a passing influence), the latter *actual grace* (transient or *actual* grace enables man to use these new habitual graces, to put them into effect in actions; the Latin word "actus" means an action). Habitual grace can mean either the basic gift of a new life and a new nature—this is *sanctifying grace*—or abiding capabilities of action expressive of this new life—the new *virtues,* such as faith, hope, and charity. God gives an actual grace, for example, to enable man to exercise the habitual grace of faith by making an act of faith.

grace $\begin{cases} \text{as the gracious reality of God himself, communicating himself to} \\ \quad \text{man: Uncreated Grace} \\ \text{as the results of God's communication to man: created graces} \end{cases}$

created graces $\begin{cases} \text{habitual—abiding gifts of God} \begin{cases} \text{sanctifying grace (man's new nature)} \\ \text{virtues (continuing powers of action)} \end{cases} \\ \text{actual—passing assistance given by God to enable man to make acts} \\ \quad \text{expressive of his new life} \end{cases}$

108 *immanent*: Catholic theology teaches that in the order of salvation God unites man to himself by communicating something of himself to man; he becomes immanent within him. God does not remain above and beyond man, but enters into him in bestowing the gifts of grace.

indwelling: God not only bestows on man the gift of sanctifying grace and the virtues, but is himself present to the justified man in a new and unique way through these gifts. Christian tradition since the New Testament has called this presence of God associated with grace *the divine indwelling*. The divine persons are present to and abide in the Christian, and are the objects of the new knowledge of faith and the new love of charity.

infused virtue: see *virtue*.

"intrinsecist": the notion, contrasted with "extrinsecist," which emphasizes that God is present within man and acts in him, and that the divine gifts of grace truly inhere in man's soul.

moral virtues: see *virtue*.

natural sonship: see *sonship*.

objectivity: the state of being an object. The object is the thing thought of, as the correlative of the thinking subject; something is considered "objectively" when it is seen as an object of thought or love. Thus God is the object of faith since he is the reality about which the act of faith is concerned. In this context the word objectivity does not mean impartially or without personal bias, but refers to the state or condition or mode of being of something which is the object of an act, especially an act of thought or love.

participation: sharing in something or in some activity. All men participate in a common humanity; all members of a team participate in a common activity. In a more philosophical sense, all things participate in reality and being. This means that they *have* both, although they do not possess either in its totality. In the order of salvation, the Christian shares in God's own life and activity; this is a true participation, for man literally takes part in what is proper to God, e.g., the act of divine knowledge by faith.

powers of action: capacities for activity. Because man is capable of the activity of thought, the mind is called a power of action in him. By learning mathematics man is made capable of mathematical thought; his knowledge of mathematics is a specialized power of action. In the order of grace, man is given powers of action which make him capable of activities beyond those he can acquire by his own efforts, e.g., thinking the thoughts of God.

redemption: the restoration of man to a condition of divine sonship by the passion and resurrection of Christ, which is mediated by the new life of grace. The redemptive effects of Christ's action are communicated to man in the Church through the sacraments, beginning with baptism.

salvation: the saving of man from sin and its effects by virtue of the passion and resurrection of Christ. Man is saved by being united with God in Christ through the bestowal of the new life of grace.

sonship: the quality of being a son or offspring, apart from male and female. With reference to God man is called a son in two senses: by creation he is the son of God; by nature he has been given being and life by his Father or Creator. By grace man becomes the son of God in a new way, being taken into the life of God in Christ. In the order of grace he is born again and becomes a

109

son in a way different from merely being the creature of the divine Creator. St. Paul speaks of the "adoption of sons" to indicate the new relation of man to God over and above his relation to him as Creator. It is called sonship because God causes a new being in man; it is called adoptive to distinguish it from the relationship of simple creature to Creator.

structure: the coordinated union of various elements to form a whole or a unit (as in a building, a skeleton, a grammatical sentence). Structure may be distinguished from meaning or function. The grammatical structure of a sentence, the anatomical structure of the body, or the architectural structure of a building may be distinguished from the function, use, and meaning of these realities. In the theology of grace, one speaks of the structure of grace and thus describes the coordinated elements which make up the life of grace: sanctifying grace, the virtues and powers of action, are structural elements in the organism of grace. The meaning and function of these structures is to unite man in his being and his activity to the life of God in Christ.

subjectivity: (correlative to objectivity or the state of being an object), the state of being a subject. In modern philosophy subjectivity usually refers to the conscious self, the thinking or knowing subject as opposed to the object thought about. Man as subject is thus the conscious center of acts directed to objects. In the act of faith man is the subject of thought, whereas God is its object. To consider faith "subjectively" means to look at faith as it is possessed by man the subject. This is correlative to thinking of faith "objectively" which would consider faith from the objects about which faith centers. Grace itself may be looked at from the point of view of subjectivity. Attention is then focused on man's possession of grace. He is its subject. God is the "object" whom grace refers to and participates in.

virtue: a capacity for good action in some area of life. Virtue is not just the capacity to act, e.g., to love; neither is it the good activity, e.g., loving. It falls between these two, being a qualification of the capacity to love (act of the will), which makes the person able to love in accordance with the moral order. It is thus a capacity to act well. In the Christian various forms of virtue are to be found: *from the point of view of their origin:* virtues are either *acquired* or *infused. Acquired* virtues are gained by man's conscious efforts. He may thus acquire a new ability to act constantly with genuine patience. *Infused* virtues are those bestowed on man not as a result of his efforts but of God's gifts. These infused virtues are given to enable man to express in good actions the life of grace; *from the point of view of their field of exercise:* theological tradition has distinguished the (infused) *theological* and the *moral* virtues. The former deal immediately with God; they share in actions which are divine and have God as their immediate object. These virtues are *faith, hope,* and *charity.* The infused moral virtues do not deal immediately with God but with the areas of daily life. These virtues are infused by God to enable man to act in a distinctively Christian way in the activities of everyday behavior. These virtues are classified under the headings of *prudence, justice, fortitude,* and *temperance.*

Selected Readings

CHAPTER ONE

Bonnetain, P., *"Grâce," Dictionnaire de la Bible, Supplément,* T.III.

Bonsirven, Joseph, *Theologie du Nouveau Testament* (Paris: Aubier, 1951), pp. 55-80, 89-109, 145-159, 287-329, 359-373, 417-423.

Dodd, C. H., *The Interpretation of the Fourth Gospel* (Cambridge: At the University Press, 1955), pp. 144-150, 187-200, 201-212.

Gleason, Robert W., *Grace* (New York: Sheed and Ward, 1962), pp. 1-66.

Grossouw, W. K., *In Christ: A Sketch of the Theology of St. Paul* (Westminster, Md.: Newman, 1952).

————, *Revelation and Redemption: A Sketch of the Theology of St. John* (Westminster, Md.: Newman, 1955).

————, *Spirituality of the New Testament* (St. Louis: B. Herder, 1961).

Guillet, J., *Themes of the Bible* (Notre Dame, Ind.: Fides, 1960).

Verity, G. B., *Life in Christ: A Study in Coinherence* (London: Longmans, Green, 1954).

CHAPTER TWO

Bouyer, Louis, *The Spirit and Forms of Protestantism* (Westminster, Md.: Newman, 1956), Ch. 1.

Gilson, Etienne, *The Christian Philosophy of St. Augustine* (New York: Random House, 1960), pp. 11-24, 143-164, 217-226.

Gleason, Robert W., *Grace* (New York: Sheed and Ward, 1962), Appendices I, II.

Grabowski, Stanislaus, *The All-Present God: A Study in St. Augustine* (St. Louis: B. Herder, 1954).

Jauncey, E., *The Doctrine of Grace up to the End of the Pelagian Controversy* (London: Macmillan, 1925).

Rondet, H., *Gratia Christi* (in French) (Paris: Beauchesne, 1948).

CHAPTER THREE

Brunner, August, *A New Creation: Towards a Theology of the Christian Life* (London: Burns and Oates, 1955), Ch. 1.

Cuttaz, F., *Our Life of Grace* (Chicago: Fides, 1958).

Daujat, Jean, "Twentieth Century Encyclopedia of Catholicism," Vol. 23, *Theology of Grace* (New York: Hawthorn Books, 1959).

Dockx, S., *Fils de Dieu par Grâce* (Paris: Desclée de Brouwer, 1948).

Galtier, Paul, *L'Habitation en nous des Trois Personnes* (Paris: Beauchesne, 1928).

Garrigou-Lagrange, Reginald, *Grace* (St. Louis: Herder, 1952).

Gleason, Robert W., *Grace* (New York: Sheed and Ward, 1962), pp. 67-187.

Hill, William J., *Proper Relations to the Indwelling Divine Persons* (Washington: Thomist Press, n.d.).

Joyce, G. H., *The Catholic Doctrine of Grace* (Westminster, Md.: Newman, 1950).

Scheeben, Matthias J., *The Glories of Divine Grace* (Cincinnati: Benziger, 1886).

————, *Nature and Grace* (St. Louis: B. Herder, 1954).

ABBREVIATIONS

The Books of the Old and New Testaments

Genesis	Gn	Canticle of Canticles	Ct
Exodus	Ex	Wisdom	Wis
Leviticus	Lv	Sirach (Ecclesiasticus)	Sir
Numbers	Nm	Isaia	Is
Deuteronomy	Dt	Jeremia	Jer
Joshua	Jos	Lamentations	Lam
Judges	Jgs	Baruch	Bar
Ruth	Ru	Ezechiel	Ez
1 Samuel (1 Kings)	1 Sm	Daniel	Dn
2 Samuel (2 Kings)	2 Sm	Osea	Os
1 Kings (3 Kings)	1 Kgs	Joel	Jl
2 Kings (4 Kings)	2 Kgs	Amos	Am
1 Chronicles (Paralipomenon)	1 Chr	Abdia	Abd
2 Chronicles (Paralipomenon)	2 Chr	Jona	Jon
Ezra	Ez	Michea	Mi
Nehemia (2 Ezra)	Neh	Nahum	Na
Tobia	Tb	Habacuc	Hb
Judith	Jdt	Sophonia	So
Esther	Est	Aggai	Ag
Job	Jb	Zacharia	Za
Psalms	Ps(s)	Malachia	Mal
Proverbs	Prv	1 Machabees	1 Mc
Coheleth (Ecclesiastes)	Coh	2 Machabees	2 Mc

In the enumeration of the Psalms, the first number follows the Vulgate, the number within brackets, the Hebrew text.

St. Matthew	Mt	1 Timothy	1 Tim
St. Mark	Mk	2 Timothy	2 Tim
St. Luke	Lk	Titus	Ti
St. John	Jn	Philemon	Phlm
Acts of the Apostles	Ac	Hebrews	Heb
Romans	Rom	St. James	Jas
1 Corinthians	1 Cor	1 St. Peter	1 Pt
2 Corinthians	2 Cor	2 St. Peter	2 Pt
Galatians	Gal	1 St. John	1 Jn
Ephesians	Eph	2 St. John	2 Jn
Philippians	Phil	3 St. John	3 Jn
Colossians	Col	St. Jude	Jude
1 Thessalonians	1 Thes	Apocalypse	Ap
2 Thessalonians	2 Thes		

Apocrypha and Qumrân Material

Henoch	Hen	Testament of the	
Jubilees	Jub	Twelve Patriarchs	Test
Psalms of Solomon	Ps Sol	Manual of Discipline	MD

Other Source Material

Acta Apostolicae Sedis
[Acts of the Apostolic See]   AAS
Ancient Christian Writers,
ed. J. Quasten and others   ACW
Acta Sanctae Sedis
[Acts of the Holy See]   ASS
Codex Iuris Canonici
[Code of Canon Law]   CIC
Denzinger-Bannwart, Enchiridion
Symbolorum, 30th ed. [Handbook
of the Creeds]   D
Patrologia, series graeca,
ed. J. P. Migne   PG
Sacrorum Conciliorum nova
. . . Collectio   Mansi

Patrologia, series latina,
ed. J. P. Migne   PL
Summa contra Gentes
S. Thomae Aquinatis   S.C.G.
Quatuor Libri Sententiarum
Petri Lombardi [Four Books
of Opinions]   Sent.
Summa Theologiae
S. Thomae Aquinatis   S.Th.
Supplementum tertiae partis Summae
Theologiae (Ottawa ed. 1941)
Suppl.
The Church Teaches,
ed. J. Clarkson and others   TCT

INDEX